OPERATION
JACKNAP

OPERATION
JACKNAP

A True Story of Kidnapping, Extortion, Ransom, and Rescue

BOMBARDIER
BOOKS

A BOMBARDIER BOOKS BOOK
An Imprint of Post Hill Press

Operation Jacknap:
A True Story of Kidnapping, Extortion, Ransom, and Rescue
© 2020 by Jack Teich
All Rights Reserved

ISBN: 978-1-64293-523-3
ISBN (eBook): 978-1-64293-524-0

Cover design by Cody Corcoran
Interior design and composition by Greg Johnson, Textbook Perfect

This is a work of nonfiction. All people, locations, events, and situations
are portrayed to the best of the author's memory.

Post Hill Press
New York • Nashville
posthillpress.com

Published in the United States of America

*I dedicate this book to my very courageous wife, Janet,
and the rest of my family.*

*In addition, the F.B.I. and Nassau County Police
Department, who were the most professional,
dedicated, compassionate individuals
that we have had the honor to know.*

Contents

Introduction

I spent years trying to lock away the memories, but the mind is a porous prison. There's no way to forget. Even now, all this time later, the images flash through my mind, bouncing from scene to scene—like light ricocheting through a labyrinth of mirrors.

Mental triggers materialize without warning. Sometimes, I'll hug my wife Janet—the one who risked everything for my rescue—and I'm transported back to the hug I gave her that fateful November day before I left for work. Dates can do it, too. Around Thanksgiving, when our children and grandkids gather at our home, a pang of panic for their safety jangles my subconscious, sending my heart hammering. Or sounds. I hear a metal chain clink or rattle, and my mind zooms me back to the closet—the cell where my abductors bound my legs and neck with metal chains, handcuffed me, and held me prisoner.

It's always there, lurking.

Through the years I developed ways to mask the trauma, tricks to project normalcy. I had to. I ran our family business, a steel fabrication company that at its peak employed 550 workers in six facilities. Knowing people depend on you forces you to hold it all together, or at least pretend to. I did the only thing I knew how: I submerged the nightmare down deep and never spoke about it. John Paul Getty III was kidnapped the year before I was, and Patty Hearst's abduction came nine months before mine. When the media called (they still do) to discuss my case or theirs, I said, "no comment." And when filmmakers sought my input on kidnapping scenes, I politely declined. I never even told our daughter, Jaime, what happened to me. I didn't want her to inherit a life of anxieties and fears. The stacks of newspaper clippings, FBI files, audio recordings, and police crime photos—I boxed it all up and hid it away.

Later, in the early 1990s, author James Patterson published the bestselling novel, *Along Came a Spider.* The book went on to become a movie starring Morgan Freeman. Even though it was fiction, Patterson had included "ripped from the headlines" accounts of famous kidnapping cases, including mine and Paul Getty's. The phone started ringing all over again. And in 1997, I found myself *still* embroiled in a courtroom battle with one of my captors, sparking even more national headlines. Nevertheless, I respectfully avoided the media spotlight and remained quiet.

Then one day I was asked to discuss my kidnapping, ransom, and rescue with a small, private group. To my own amazement, I agreed to do it. I'm glad I did. Voicing my story proved cathartic. More importantly, others were moved by what I had to say. Bringing encouragement and support to survivors and people who've endured traumatic experiences helped me reclaim a little inner peace.

My hope for you is that my story will serve as a reminder of all you cherish and hold most dear in your life. My wife, my brothers Buddy and Eddie, my father Joe, the FBI agents and Nassau County police who lived with us, and the hundreds of law enforcement officers who were assigned to operation "Jacknap" all put their lives on the line to achieve justice and ensure my safe return. Their bravery, love, and devotion are the reasons I'm alive today. This book is my way of thanking them and God for saving my life.

1

The Driveway

Rain drizzled on the windshield of my 1971 Lincoln coupe as I drove home from work at dusk.

At the stop sign blocks from my Long Island home, my eyes darted to the rear view mirror. Headlights from a trailing car shined low through the droplets streaking my rear window. It was somewhat unusual. I'd made that stop hundreds of times along the lazy route leading to my King's Point house on Ballantine Lane. Seldom, if ever, was there a car behind me. I kept driving.

When I pulled into the leaf-strewn driveway of our brown, wood-shingled, craftsman-style home, I parked about three feet away from our white two-car garage. A basketball hoop hung above it. It was 6:40 p.m., Tuesday, November 12, 1974.

I killed the headlights. Something wasn't right. I'd pushed the headlights off, but the face of the garage door still glowed. I wrenched my neck around. A car was behind mine, its headlamps

1

beaming like a spotlight. I stepped out of my car and shut the door. A voice rang out.

"Excuse me, you know how to get to Northern Boulevard?"

I squinted. The voice came from an approaching silhouette, backlit by two blasts of bright light.

"Excuse me?" I said.

A man appeared in the driveway. He was about five feet, seven inches tall, black, wore a light tan jacket and gloves, a dark green ski mask, and had a silver long-barrel pistol.

"Come on, you're coming with us. Get over here, or we're going to blow your head off," he demanded. "Now!"

I froze.

Dart into the woods behind the house, I thought for a second. *No, no...he'll go into our house.* I couldn't let that happen. Inside sat my young wife, Janet, thirty, and our two small boys. Marc was almost seven years old; Michael was just twenty-seven months.

Go with him—draw him away from the home, I told myself.

He hustled me back to a small, two-door sports car. Beside it stood a taller, thinner black man, 5'10," also wearing a dark green ski mask, with a shotgun.

The man with the handgun unlatched the door.

"Get in the back seat."

As my head breached the car's door frame, I noticed it had light-colored interior with piping on the upholstery. There was also a chrome trim on the windows.

"Lay on your side. Down."

The taller man was the driver. In the driveway was the first and only time he ever spoke to me.

"Get down! We'll blow your head off!"

I hurried onto my side and scrunched into a fetal position. My head was behind the passenger's seat, my feet toward the driver's side.

In front of me on the floorboard lay a pungent metal gasoline can.

The men jumped in the car and slapped handcuffs on me, removed my glasses, and mashed two large patches of putty over my eyes. A different pair of glasses was then slid onto my face. They left my raincoat and brown suit jacket on me. They then pulled a large sheet of cardboard over my body as we rolled away from my home.

"What do you think we are going to do with you?" the man in the passenger seat asked.

I'd spotted the gasoline can, and I felt the flammable cardboard covering my body. I tried not to let my mind go there.

"I don't know," I replied. "Rob me?"

"That's right. We're going to rob you. We are taking you up to the black side of town. We're going to take you to an abandoned tenement. You're gonna give us twenty minutes to leave. Then you can go."

Before I could stop myself, the words escaped my mouth: "Why didn't you just rob me in the driveway?"

"Don't tell me how to run my business!" he yelled. "We do it my way!"

About fifteen minutes into the drive, the car slowed to a stop. I heard the clink of two coins. A toll booth. There were only a couple like it within fifteen to twenty minutes of my house. *Maybe it's the Whitestone Bridge,* I thought. *Or maybe the Throgs Neck Bridge.* Both bridges span the East River and connect a northeastern part of Long Island to the Bronx—not far from Rikers Island.

Then again, it could be the Triborough Bridge, now named the RFK Bridge, I thought. If so, that would mean we were headed in a totally different direction; the Triborough is part of a major traffic artery connecting Queens to East Harlem.

Which bridge is it? I wondered.

I couldn't tell.

As the car sped away from the toll booth, noxious fumes from the gasoline can filled my nostrils. I tried to steady my breathing.

No sudden movements, I told myself. *Stay still.*

"What's your name?" the passenger asked.

"Jack."

"Jack Teich, right?"

"Yes."

"You're a *Jew*, right?"

"Um...yes."

What kind of question was that? What did my religion have to do with a robbery? My mind whirred.

Another fifteen minutes passed. Other than the commands from the talker in the passenger seat, the car was dead silent. No radio, no chatter between them, nothing except the occasional slosh from the gas can in front of my face.

Outside the car, something was changing. The weight of my body began rolling toward the back of the vehicle.

We're going up a hill, I thought. *A very steep hill.*

Minutes later, the car stopped.

"Don't move," the man in the passenger seat said.

He pressed his pistol against my head. My heart hammered.

"Sit there and keep quiet."

The upholstery was now slick with sweat from my face.

"We have to wait for the street to clear to take you out of the car," he said.

The smell from the gasoline can was getting to me. I dared not move. After approximately ten minutes with a gun to my head, my captor put what felt like rags over my handcuffs.

"We have to wait for one last little old lady to move out of the block," he said.

We waited.

"OK, we're getting out. I'm going to guide you, tell you how many steps to take."

The passenger door opened. He grabbed my arm to pull me out and over the gas can until I had my feet on the street. Then he called out the number of paces to take, in which direction, and when to step up.

As I took steps blindly, haunting thoughts entered my mind. *Were there others, or just these two men? Was there another car somewhere behind or in front of us? And Janet and our boys—what's happening to them?! What if there were more masked men violating my home and my family?*

* * *

BACK AT THE HOUSE, JANET WAS JUST DISCOVERING my absence. I was later than she expected, and being late in itself was somewhat unusual. She was waiting to go to the movies with her friend, Joan, and didn't want to miss the opening scenes.

She fed Marc and Michael and took them upstairs for bedtime while keeping an eye on the driveway. When she came down, she noticed my Lincoln parked in its usual spot. But I was nowhere to be found. Curious, she stepped outside.

"Jack?" Janet called out. "Honey, I'm going to be late."

There were plenty of benign reasons why I may not have come inside right away, but she sensed that none of it added up. I wasn't in the car. I wasn't near the car. I wasn't answering her call. I was there but not there—not anymore. Something was wrong.

Janet and her friend, Joan, would not be going to the movies. Instead, Joan and her husband, Barry, came over to console Janet. She was scared. Confused. Maybe there was a perfectly good explanation, and she was overreacting. They talked through multiple scenarios. Time kept ticking.

"I can't take it anymore," Janet huffed. "I'm calling the police."

Kings Point has its own local police department. Janet informed them I was missing. Several officers came to our house. She explained again that my car was in the driveway, but I was missing. The officers perused our home, ostensibly looking for clues. But they had already solved the mystery, erroneously, as it were.

Janet, near panicked, sat with Joan and Barry as the uniformed officers strolled around the house. At one point Barry saw them snickering and whispering. "They don't think anything is wrong. They're laughing at you for thinking something bad happened to Jack," Barry said under his breath. Janet tried not to fidget while awaiting the officers' briefing.

"Missus Teich, is there a possibility that your husband could've gone next door?"

"No, no I don't think so. Why would he do that? He knew Joan and I were going to see *Gone With the Wind*...he was planning to stay home and watch our boys. He wouldn't want us to be late."

"Missus Teich, your neighbor, are you aware she's gone to the airport? Would your husband have any reason to go with her? Any reason at all?"

"No reason at all. He wouldn't do that!"

Their conclusion: I must be having an affair with my neighbor's wife, Ellen, and skipped town with her. But they were wrong. Dead wrong. Janet wasn't some naïve Long Island housewife living in sub-urban denial. She knew me. I was coming home to watch our boys. And I don't blow off my family.

As the Kings Point police dropped the ball in those early hours, Janet launched her own investigation. She called all of our neighbors. None of them had seen me. She then dialed my close friend, Dick, to see if he would come over and examine my car. Dick and I often rode into the city together. Being a creature of habit, she hoped he might find something out of place. As Janet's panicked mind raced with scenarios of what may have happened, she felt certain I would have left some sort of clue in the car, signaling foul play. But Dick came up empty.

By now, it had been dark for some time. Janet enlisted her father and our friend, Seymour, to tromp through our soggy, leaf-blanketed neighborhood. They looked everywhere. Then a chilling thought went through her like a spear: *What if Jack has been stuffed in a gar-bage can in our shed?*

They hadn't looked there. Not yet. Janet was too terrified to look. Her father volunteered for the potentially gruesome task. He walked resolutely to the shed. When he put his hand on the shed handle, he exhaled to prepare himself for what he might discover.

* * *

MEANWHILE, BACK ON THE STREET in God-knows-where, one of my abductors was marching me into a building like a prison guard escorting a blind inmate.

We repeated the ill-fated dance as he muttered directions to me. Forward together, him leading, a tight squeeze and more steps. An awkward tango. We came to a landing, probably a stoop, I thought. We walked inside. More steps and stairs as he gripped my arm. Maybe thirty stairs in all until we reached a door. *Zip, clink, rack*, the first lock was keyed and opened. Then the next. A few steps more, and we were inside a room. The floor creaked as my dress shoes clacked against it. The door shut behind me like a sealed vault.

The car ride had been harrowing, but at least in a moving car there were other people all around who could see and hear something. But now? All I knew was that I was standing in some sort of building far removed from my surroundings, walled off from the eyes and ears of anyone who might help me escape.

I had no idea who these people were, whether they intended to rob me as they claimed or something worse. Only one thing was certain: this nightmare was just beginning.

2

The Closet

Standing there, handcuffed and blinded, a hand thrust down into my breast pocket.

"Shut up," he said, though I hadn't said anything. It was the passenger—the man I would come to think of as my "Keeper." His fingers frittered about, grasping for whatever he could find. He moved to the next outside pocket on my raincoat, and then the next. He was methodical, systematic. He searched the inside pockets, top to bottom. Then my suit jacket. Then pants. There would be no mistakes.

I tried to stand still but flinched as he jarred me off balance with each probing pocket grab. He vacuumed my pockets of everything— money, a pen, my tie, an eyeglass case, my Seiko watch, and two uncashed paychecks.

"Oh, so you treat yourself pretty good, don't you," he said while riffling the $1,200 folded in my money clip. I didn't even try to explain that the cash was for an upcoming family vacation we were planning, because we rarely used a credit card.

Once he had everything, it sounded like he walked into another room. I could hear him walking, then fiddling with what I guessed was a canvas bag. I heard the *zooot* of the zipper and his hands rubbing around the inside of the bag making that distinct canvas sound. I could hear him moving around and shifting things.

"I've got something else in store for you," he said.

What the hell does that mean? I thought.

Had he lied about letting me go twenty minutes after robbing me? Or was there now a sudden change of plans? On some level I knew the answer—things were about to get a lot worse.

The room then filled with the rattle of metal chains.

What's happening?! I thought, now fearing the worst.

A pile dropped in front of me and crashed with a metallic thud. I felt something being wrapped around my ankle. A padlock clicked shut. The Keeper then snaked the chain over and around my other ankle. Back and forth, in and out, up my legs. Another padlock clicked. I braced myself and tried to remain still like a statue. The last thing I wanted was to trigger a violent reaction.

He grabbed my arm and guided me across the room. My chains clattered and clanked as my bound legs shuffled forward. My head bumped something small that started jingling. A metal hanger? My kidnapper moved it away and pushed me to the ground.

"Sit down on the floor," he commanded.

My hands were still cuffed. Another chain clacked as it was run through what must have been an eye hook bored into the foot of a closet. A closet—that would be my new prison cell. It was a tight, three-sided space that was too small and cramped to be much else.

"Lie down on your back," he said, using his foot to push me to the floor.

I laid there blind, exposed, and resting supine with my head facing the ceiling. He then went to work. I crossed my arms over my body in case he decided to unleash a flurry of punches or kicks.

He then roped another chain around my neck before securing it to the eye hook on the closet wall. *Click*, another padlock.

Why is this happening?! Why all this for a simple robbery? Why me?

"I see your credit is good all over town," he said. "We still got more in store for you."

His fingers clawed and dug into the putty covering my eyes. Once off, darkness. *That's strange*, I thought. Then I remembered it was nighttime, and the lights in the room must've been off. I couldn't see anything, but I could smell the gasoline from the car on his gloves.

The next thing I felt was a thick adhesive bandage being wound around my head. Then he gagged me. I was terrified of suffocating. I tried to calm my racing heart; triggering a coughing episode could induce a panic attack or choking.

He left the room.

I'm not going to make it...Don't think that! STOP! I told myself.

He reentered the room a few minutes later and removed the gag. A rare moment of relief. But then I realized the reason why he took the gag out of my mouth. He didn't do it for me. He did it for the interrogation.

* * *

"WHAT'S YOUR WIFE'S NAME? How many children do you have? What are their names? How old are they? How many brothers do you have? What are their names? How old are they? Where do they live? What are their phone numbers?"

The Keeper wanted to know everything.

"Here," he said. "Drink." He pushed a straw into my mouth as I slurped a few gulps of lukewarm water. He then launched into another withering barrage of questions.

I felt torn. This person, this demented criminal had no business knowing anything about my family. I would never put my family in harm's way, but I had to comply. I had no choice. I had to tell him what he wanted to hear. I had to survive—for the family. An outright refusal to answer could be met with swift punishment.

I rattled off names, ages, addresses, and phone numbers as best I could, thinking a subtle mistake here or there, like a seven instead of an eight within a ten-digit phone number, would go unnoticed. I skipped details about my brother, Buddy, as I recited a litany of identifying facts about other people and things. "He lives in the City," I said, and just moved on. I didn't tell his address and assumed my captor didn't notice. But he knew. He later told me exactly what Buddy's address was.

"What kind of cars do you have? What kinds of cars do your brothers have? Where do you vacation? Do you have maids? A butler? How much is the mortgage on your house? What kind of mortgage is it?"

He asked if I owned stocks. "What kind? How much are they worth?"

The questions were so thorough, they seemed ridiculous at times.

"Do you own any antiques? What kind? How much are they worth? Tell me about them. How about artwork? Do you own any artwork? What kind? How much?"

Antiques? Seriously? What street thug thinks about stealing art and antiques? But the answer was, yes. I kept some art in my home and in my office.

I answered the questions the best I could, minimizing details wherever possible. If the information was obvious, such as the type of cars in my driveway, I told him everything I knew. But when I guessed he couldn't know a full answer, I tried to divulge as little as possible. It was a dangerous game. Like a skilled attorney, he asked several questions whose answers he already knew. He was testing me. The quality and granularity of his inquisition made one thing crystal clear: he knew a lot more about me than he let on.

"How much do you get paid?" he asked.

He knew the answer. He had already taken my paychecks.

11

"Seven hundred dollars net, twelve hundred dollars gross," I said.

"And two paychecks? You pay yourself well!" he said in a half-mock, half-scold.

"How much money do you have in your bank account?" he asked.

"Um, I have five thousand dollars at the Banker's Trust Company," I said.

"What other money do you take out of the company?" he said. "How much?"

The company?

"What do you guys make at your company?"

"Steel doors," I said.

"Steel doors?" He thought that was funny. He didn't laugh, but it amused him.

"How many people?" he asked.

"Um, there's about a hundred people on the payroll," I answered.

"What about profits? What are the profits? How much is your machinery worth? Are you going to expand?"

"We'll spend about twenty thousand dollars on machinery by year's end," I told him. "It's hard to know profits right now."

"It's a union shop. We pay union wages," I volunteered.

"Union?" he said. He seemed surprised.

"How many buildings do you own or rent? Would your wife call the police if you didn't come home?"

"Yes," I answered.

"What would you get from your brother?" he asked.

"What?"

"What are your in-laws worth?" he said.

"I don't know. They're working people," I said.

"Working people," he muttered before getting up and leaving the room.

I lay in the blackness straining to listen. Then the thought came zooming at me again like a bullet train: *there is no way you're getting out of here alive.* A searing image as if from a horror film began forming in my mind. Me in the closet...the Keeper standing beside it...the head of a match dragging along a strike plate...the Keeper tossing the lit match into the closet....me writhing and screaming as my corpse is engulfed in flames.

Shaking the macabre image from my mind proved futile. Throughout my captivity, the grisly scene of being cremated alive replayed itself as if on a feedback loop.

The sound of shuffling feet snapped my mind to attention.

"What do you mean that they're *working* people?" the Keeper barked as he reentered the room.

He was back in interrogation mode.

"Who's the strongest and who's the weakest of your brothers?" he asked.

"I don't know," I said.

He asked about my brother's wife. "How much control does Lois have over Buddy? Can he make decisions without her?"

"Um, I suppose. Yeah, sure."

My nerves were frazzled. The physical, emotional, and psychological stress was building to a breaking point. I was starting to crack.

"Take whatever you want. Please! Don't drag this out anymore," I blurted out in between questions. Bad move.

"Don't tell me what to do! Don't you EVER tell me what to do! I tell you! Got it? I tell you! You don't tell me anything! Don't you ever tell me ANYTHING!"

He stormed out of the room.

I'd messed up. Bad.

* * *

THE KEEPER CAME BACK A SHORT TIME LATER.

"You're going to make a tape," he announced.

It was late. Even though I was traumatized and barely hanging on, he wasn't tired in the least. He was just getting warmed up. He came to the closet and knelt down next to me.

"You're going to say exactly what I tell you to say. And it better be convincing. Understand? You'll never see your family again if it's not convincing, I promise you that," he said.

I had no reason not to believe him.

He held a small microphone to my lips and told me what to say and how to say it. He wanted money. That was the bottom line.

He was getting frustrated with me, clicking a tape recorder button on and off. "You're too nervous," he said. "You're not convincing. Don't make it sound like we have a gun to your head."

I started over, but it wasn't working.

"Run it again!" he said.

He put the microphone in my cuffed hand. "You hold it," he said. It was small, plastic, and connected by a wire back to the tape recorder. There was an on/off switch on the mic. He told me to flip it up or down to pause the tape and start recording again, but I had trouble remembering if up or down was on or vice versa. He kept getting more upset. He would also stop the tape intermittently and press me for more information. It was too much.

He drilled down for details about Janet. Then Buddy's wife. Then a new round of questions: "Who's stronger, your wife or Buddy's wife? Who's weaker? Who gets excited? Who do you think we should contact?"

I tried to keep up.

Finally, it was over.

"Ok, we'll go with that."

My head slunk limp. He left the room again. He was done with me, for now.

* * *

THE NEXT MORNING, THE KINGS POINT POLICE insisted that Janet go to our bank to see if I'd withdrawn any money. If I had, it would lend credence to their theory that I'd skipped town with our neighbor, Ellen. *Absurd.* They had other theories: I had gotten drunk and stayed out all night; I'd taken a train, it was delayed, and I never called. Janet knew it was all bunk. To my delight, I later found out that she took them only to our local bank and nowhere near where we kept our main accounts. They weren't serious; involving them deeper into our affairs at that point was only inviting unnecessary distractions.

Once they saw there had been no withdrawals, the Kings Point police took her a little more seriously, but they had no plan. Sure, the situation was odd. Nothing like this had ever happened in our town, but they still treated Janet like a clueless housewife. They couldn't have been more wrong.

Janet hadn't slept. She was desperate and irritated that the police weren't listening to her. She wanted them to believe her. She knew me. My love for her and our sons was absolute. She needed help. Somehow, she had the wherewithal to think of my old friend, Jed Orenstein. Jed and I had known each other since we were young kids; our families were friends. He knew me very well, and he was now an assistant district attorney. He confirmed Janet's innermost beliefs, that I would never simply not come home without a word.

Jed immediately called Nassau County Police Chief Ed Curran. "Ed, I have known the family and Jack Teich since he was four years old, and this is totally out of character for Jack. There is something very wrong here." NCPD police officers and detectives soon showed up at our house by the carload. The cavalry had arrived.

The Nassau detectives launched their own interrogation. They, too, wanted to know everything, but from Janet. At one point, she volunteered that I might have been killed and was perhaps floating in a nearby neighbor's pool. There had been much gossip in the neighborhood that a particular gentleman who lived there was involved with the mafia. I've never had anything to do with something like that, and it makes no sense looking back, but desperation is a funny thing. It was a frantic attempt to ensure that no stone was left unturned—or pool unsearched.

Janet was friendly with the man's wife, Jan. Our sons played together. The police questioned him and, of course, he knew nothing of my disappearance. A senior detective then demanded to see my car. Janet informed him it hadn't moved since the previous night and that the Kings Point police had already searched it inside and outside for clues. Saying the same things over and over again was irksome.

"Look, my husband left for work in the morning, and he always comes home, give or take, around 7:00 p.m."

She was double-stepping to keep up with the detective as he traversed across the yard. "We looked in Jack's car already," Janet repeated.

He stopped and stared into her eyes. "Missus Teich, I'm not leaving here until I've popped open that trunk," he said.

The subtext of his words hit her like a truck. These men had seen things no one ever should. They had committed their lives to confronting human depravity so the rest of us could live in peace. They are the wall between the civilized and criminal worlds. Those worlds now intersected at the trunk of my car.

Janet's heart was in her throat. *Oh no...oh no...please...this can't be how this ends*, she thought. She sucked in a deep breath. The detective slid the key into the lock, twisted it to the right, and popped open the trunk.

No bloodied corpse. Nothing.

Janet exhaled and got back to work. By now, the house was filled with uniformed police officers and plain-clothes detectives. They stayed well into the evening. They continued searching the neighborhood and woods behind our house. They looked carefully for anything that might provide a lead. Wet, trampled leaves soon covered the kitchen floor, an odd visual account of the many people coming in and out of our home that painful evening. A tape recorder was set up in the kitchen. Little did they know how soon it would be needed.

* * *

BACK IN THE CLOSET, I HAD TO RELIEVE MYSELF. The Keeper plunked a plastic pail outside my closet that popped with a hollow plastic sound as it hit the floor. It was lined with a plastic bag. He placed it close enough that I could pull it towards me with the slack in my chains.

"Do your business in there," said the Keeper.

My hands remained cuffed, and my legs and neck were still chained to the closet walls, but there was just enough slack to wiggle into a strained kneel. It was a filthy process.

Later, the Keeper brought cans of juice and snacks and put them next to the foul bucket.

The interrogation resumed.

"How do Janet and Lois get along? Who should go with Buddy to drop the money?"

"Janet," I said. "She'll know what to do."

"If your kids got hurt, would Janet get hysterical?" he asked.

"Yes. Yes. She would," I said, trembling.

"What about your father? How much would he give for you?"

"He's very sick," I said. *Please, please leave my father in peace.*

"Does your father take vacations? How can he afford vacations? Is he on Social Security? What about income-producing properties? Does he have any? What about you, do you have any? How many? How much can you get for them?"

He was so curious about how we made money, but it didn't seem specific to us. He genuinely didn't know how to make a lot of money. He was curious, but it was all wrong.

The Keeper showed a renewed interest in our family business.

"What's your sales volume?" he asked.

"About six million dollars gross," I answered—an understatement.

"I can explain how it works," I offered gingerly. He didn't say anything. I took a deep breath and started on about inflation and growth, that sales revenue isn't liquid cash in the bank that can be withdrawn at any time. "There are expenses and taxes and other obligations involved in running a business," I said.

He interrupted me with his own strange teaching about real estate. A few minutes in and it dawned on me that I had left a real estate report in my jacket pocket that I had forgotten about. He must have read it cover-to-cover. He was eager to talk about it. I was surprised how much he understood. He was bright, I'll give him that. The report was an opinion written by an attorney from a real estate investment group I was involved in. It was fairly complicated, so the Keeper asked a lot of questions.

"I see you're looking to buy a foreclosure deal in California," he said.

"Yes. My share is small, just a ten-thousand-dollar interest," I told him.

He thought I was making money, but as I explained, almost the entire investment was a complete loss. I was losing money on it. It was the truth.

"Jew slumlords," he said under his breath.

"Your money is going overseas to buy food for poor people," he said in a non-sequitur.

"Come again?" I said.

"Are you in the J.D.L [Jewish Defense League]?" he asked. "How much do you and your family give to the JDL?"

My stomach churned with uneasiness. "I don't understand," I responded. I got the impression he might be involved with a Palestinian movement of some kind.

"How much money do you give to the JDL?!" he repeated, insisting that the Jews were going to kill Arafat. He was obsessed.

Yasser Arafat, or Mohammed Yasser Abdel Rahman Abdel Raouf Arafat al-Qudwa al-Husseini, was a Palestinian political leader who had been the chairman of the Palestine Liberation Organization since 1969. Arafat was an avowed enemy of Israel who died several decades later in old age. None of that stuff had anything to do with me. I was a Jewish family guy who worked in Brooklyn and lived on Long Island.

"How much money did you give to the JDL?" he asked again. "You're going to kill Arafat. You watch," he said.

I stopped responding. He was satisfied just to humiliate me. Then he dropped two cellophane bags of salted peanuts next to my head and left the room.

Later, he came back again. He couldn't resist. He wanted to know more about my family business, although it was less theoretical this time and more fact-finding.

"How many bank accounts do you have at your company?" he asked.

"Two," I told him. "One is a general account, and one is a payroll account."

"How much money do you keep in the accounts?"

"Fifty thousand, total," I said.

He left the room again and didn't return. Not for a long time. I laid on the floor, bound in darkness, and thought of home.

* * *

THAT NIGHT, OUR HOME TELEPHONE RANG at 9:13 p.m. A detective told Janet earlier that if I was alive, someone might call and that they should be ready. It was a blunt thing to say to a young mother, but it was one of many precautionary statements made that day as the law enforcement world moved in and enveloped our white picket fence existence.

As instructed, Janet waited a few rings before picking up so the detectives could begin recording the call. She hovered over the telephone and waited for a signal. A detective nodded toward her. "Ok, go," he said.

Janet picked up.

"Hello"

"Janet?" a male voice said.

"Yes?" she said, hesitantly.

"Jack is safe, and he's alive. If you want to see him again...seven hundred and fifty thousand dollars. We will call you tomorrow."

She waived frantically to the detectives.

"Wait! What?!" she said.

The detectives inched toward her, leaning in ears first.

"You will be called tomorrow. Seven hundred and fifty thousand," the voice said. Then, dial tone.

She was in shock. She panned the room and stared at the men in her house, telephone still in hand, mouth agape. "He hung up," she said.

Was that real? Am I in a movie? This doesn't happen to people like us, Janet thought.

It was a ransom call. The first one. It didn't surprise the detectives or the FBI agents who had now joined the effort to find me. The required sum, however, did surprise them. It was one of the largest ransom demands ever in the United States up to that time. The mystery of my disappearance had been solved. I wasn't out drinking, and there was no promiscuous affair with some neighbor. I'd been kidnapped.

John Paul Getty III was kidnapped in Italy a year earlier and held for $17 million. Patty Hearst was kidnapped months earlier by the Symbionese Liberation Army, a violent militant group. Two armed men took the 19-year-old Hearst from her apartment in Berkeley, California, and demanded millions for her return. She was later convicted of bank robbery and using a gun during a crime. In 2001, she was pardoned by President Bill Clinton.

The gravity of my kidnapping—a Long Island businessman— was also sinking in for the Nassau County detectives and FBI agents. Seven hundred and fifty thousand dollars—the equivalent of $4 million today. The logistics of coming up with that kind of money, let alone delivering it and planning and executing necessary law enforcement operations, would be immense.

The ransom call brought a flood of emotions for Janet. The brutal cruelty of twenty-six hours of fear and panic, not knowing where I was and what was happening to me was absolute terror. Hearing that I was alive brought relief and vindication that I hadn't run off with the neighbor's wife. That horrific twenty-six-hour wait had gifted us something valuable though...the recorded call. Had they called much earlier, the recorder would not have been in place. Trying to comprehend it all made her lightheaded.

Feeling alone and not knowing what to do, Janet called Buddy, my oldest brother. He came to the house to comfort her with his wife, Lois. My middle brother, Edwin, also came over, as did Janet's parents, Arnold and Sylvia Rosenberg. They all rushed to console her. Next came my father, Joseph, the patriarch, then my uncle Harvey, my aunt Helen, and their daughter, Marlene. It was an outpouring of family love and support.

But Janet had no intention of sitting *shiva*—a Jewish ritual for mourning the death of a loved one. She believed in her heart that I would come back. Her resolve still amazes me. The ransom call was devastating, but the caller said I was alive. She wouldn't allow herself to think otherwise. It was the only way not to fall apart. I was alive, at least for now. The kidnapper wanted money. As far as Janet was concerned, it was up to her to make the exchange and get me back. Her mind was made up: her husband was coming home.

Janet refused to cry in front of anyone, whether family or police. If she started, she thought she might not be able to stop. *I need to stay strong for the payoff,* she told herself. In her mind she envisioned the moment when we would be reunited. In her own unique way, Janet was determined not to be a basket case for my return, feeling it would devastate me to see her like that. Instead, her tears fell in private that night as she held our sleeping two-year-old son, Michael, tight in her arms.

The detectives stayed throughout the night, as did the FBI. Unsure if there would be another call, Janet slept in her clothes to be ready at a moment's notice for whatever came next.

3

The Bed

I clung to the concept of time the best I could. I tried to measure the passing of days and nights, hours and minutes. The mental anguish and psychological strain made it hard to keep my grip on reality. A thud from above? An upstairs neighbor dropped something. Or did the sound come from somewhere else? The next room? My own mind? Did I imagine it? Did it matter? Does anything matter if I don't get out of here alive? I kept thinking the whole place a tinderbox. What's to stop the Keeper from torching it once he gets his money? *That's what the gasoline is for, I bet.* To destroy the evidence, and I'm the biggest clue.

I pushed my thoughts to wander beyond my chains and fixate on my family. Like a slide projector in my head, each face flashed before me. Janet, Marc, Michael—I loved them dearly and longed for their presence. What would happen to them without me? What would happen to them if these bastards killed me? It wasn't a farfetched outcome. I wanted to spare my boys the pain and confusion of growing up without a father. I hadn't even grasped that they could also grow up without a mother, but that was very much a possibility. Then a wave of resolve washed over me. *This beautiful family is worth living for. Stay strong for them.* It was the greatest solace. They were worth living for. Somehow, some way, I was going to see them again. Holding fast to the hope of reunification with my family—that was my tether to survival and sanity.

Boom!

Without warning, the Keeper burst into the room.

A jolt of electricity went through my body; my chains jumped to life.

"If a building inspector or mailman comes in the building [which happened a couple times] keep your mouth shut."

He put a straw in my mouth. A few sips. It was room temperature and tasted chlorinated. *Borough tap water,* I thought.

"You want food?" he asked.

"No." *Is it morning?*

He noticed I hadn't eaten anything from the day before. "Hey, we don't waste food here," he barked. "You understand? I won't bring it if you don't eat it."

He dropped a roll of toilet paper next to my head and began straightening the room. I could hear him. It was a big deal to keep the room orderly, which was ironic given the plastic bodily waste pail and the human being he kept shackled in the closet.

The Keeper gave me a handheld radio. It boosted my morale. But was it to pass the time, or mask conversation in the next room? Everything he did was for his benefit, not mine. I was a thing. A means to an end. Still, I was losing the energy to be repulsed by his wickedness. I was getting used to my conditions, but I couldn't allow exhaustion to wear down my sense of right and wrong. *I can't accept this. I can detach, but I can't stop caring,* I thought. *He'll never convince me that I've done anything to deserve this.*

When he left the room, I wiggled my aching body into position, negotiating the slack in the chains, and relieved myself. It was humiliating.

* * *

A WHILE LATER THE KEEPER BURST INTO THE ROOM AGAIN, this time irate.

"You didn't tell me about the third account! You didn't tell me!"

"I don't know. I don't understand," I said.

"The third account! The employee account!"

He said he'd talked to Buddy and that our company had an account with a lot of money in it that I didn't tell him about when he interrogated me the day before. He thought I had betrayed him.

The third account, or the employee retirement account, as he called it, was a profit-sharing plan for our employees. The Keeper was furious at the omission.

"I didn't say anything because you wanted to know about my money," I said. "The employee account is not my money. It belongs to the employees."

"Don't you lie to me, or you'll end up like the other guy who lied!" he said. "We picked up a guy—had forty bucks in his pocket. We squeezed him and got four hundred thousand dollars. But he lied. Don't you dare lie."

I paused and took a long, slow inhale, then said, again, "It belongs to the employees. It's the truth."

"How much money is in it?" he asked.

"I don't know. I really don't know," I answered.

"How do you not know?! Who signs the checks?"

"I do," I said.

He was thinking. I thought this could be one of those times when he knew the answer to his question and was testing me.

"I do," I repeated. "I sign the checks."

"Well, if you sign the checks then how do you not know how much money is in it?!"

"I just started signing checks for that account, and it needs two signatures," I said.

"Who else? Who else signs the checks?" he asked.

"Buddy and me," I said.

He probably figured I was lying, but he couldn't know for sure. He didn't know how large businesses worked. He wanted to know but didn't. It confounded him. It made him angry that people he hated were more successful than he was. He couldn't do it, so I had to be corrupt. I was exploitative and deceitful. That was the only way to explain his unfulfilled desires to himself. His failures were my fault.

"If you were on the outside, and we had your brother in here, how much money could you get?" he said.

I had to think about it. I had to weigh what he would believe and what I could explain.

"Um, two hundred thousand dollars? If I sold everything and scraped together everything I could, I could maybe get two hundred thousand dollars."

He stormed off but came back later wanting to know more. This time he was calm.

"So, where do you keep the money in the employee account?" he asked.

"It belongs to the employees, and the money is invested in stocks and bonds," I said. "You can't just go to a bank and withdraw it. It's invested."

He exhaled. He was frustrated.

"Do you do as badly with their money as you do with your own?" he sniped before leaving the room in a huff. I gathered it was a reference to the real estate investment I was losing money on. I would later learn that real estate was his defunct passion, and that his knowledge of the company profit-sharing fund didn't come from Buddy, but a former employee.

* * *

THAT NIGHT, THE PHONE RANG AGAIN at 2 Ballantine Lane. Janet had asked our close friends and family not to call the house. It was critical to keep the line open. She also asked them not to say anything about the kidnapping until the police gave the go-ahead. My life depended on it. By now, people in the neighborhood had to know something was wrong. The signs were everywhere, but they were left to guess. Inside the house, however, there was relative clarity. There was only one thing to do: wait. Wait for the kidnappers to call. And at 9:55 p.m. on Thursday, November 14, they did.

As before, Janet let it ring a few times before picking up. She had barely slept or eaten since Tuesday night. It didn't matter. Not now. She had to step up. The detectives and agents took their marks. Someone clicked a record button. "And...go."

"Hello," Janet answered.

"Hello, Janet there?" a male voice said.

"Yes, this is Janet."

"Tell Buddy to go to the Exxon Station—"

"Wait! Wait, please."

"Tell Buddy—"

"No, please. I can't remember. Is Jack ok?" she asked.

"Stop talking and listen," the voice said over her. "Tell Buddy to go to the Exxon station around the corner from his house. There is a trash can and inside it is a message for Buddy."

"Buddy's here, will you speak to him?" she asked.

"No. A message from Jack—"

"Is Jack ok?" she asked, again.

"There is a message from Jack...in the garbage bag...inside the trash can...at the Exxon station around the corner from Buddy's house. He must get that immediately. All of the information is in the bag."

Janet tried to make the caller stay on the phone as she'd been coached by law enforcement, but she was frantic and wanted to hear from me.

"A message from Buddy?" she asked. "Speak to Buddy, he's right here. I can't remember."

"Stop talking and listen!" the caller responded.

"Is Jack ok? Can I talk to him?" she asked, but he hung up.

She looked around for direction. An extended silence was broken when it was announced that the call was untraceable. "He wasn't on long enough," someone said.

My brother Buddy got moving. The police and FBI weren't going to risk a nighttime commercial garbage pickup. Buddy left Kings Point, Long Island, in his 1974 silver Pontiac and traveled north on a similar path the kidnappers had used forty-eight hours ago. But instead of exiting into New York City, he continued on to Larchmont, a coastal town along the north side of the Long Island Sound. Nassau County police and the FBI followed in tow.

At 11:40 p.m., Buddy arrived at the Exxon station on Boston Post Road and parked next to a garbage barrel at the front of the service station. He had no idea if he was being watched. Buddy pulled out a dark green plastic bag. He got back into his car and drove to a place where the contents could safely be examined. Inspector Andrew Mulrain of the Nassau County Police Department joined him. They both took stock of the items in the bag: a black satchel, a black Dynotape cassette, a pen, a watch, a tie, an eyeglass case, dimes, quarters, and a small white envelope.

Mulrain exited the vehicle a few minutes later and told Buddy to go home. Mulrain and the others followed him some distance behind. They would all study the contents of the plastic bag into the early hours of Friday morning

The white envelope contained a letter from the kidnappers. Here is what it said:

Jack is alive and safe for now. His arrest is due to crimes against poor people. Pay his fine of $750,000 or he will be executed. If your corrupt police get involved and attempts are made to trap us, Jack will die. Then the entire family becomes targets. You are being watched. We

are able to detect radio/electronic devices. We will test your sincerity and obedience. No harm will come to any of you if you cooperate fully. No further warning. Put $700,000 in $100s, $40,000 in $20s and $10,000 in $10s in this bag. Old bills not in series. Let no one mark or record. Bertram and Janet, prepare to drive the BMW downtown in four days. Janet, wear a white head scarf. Release will be one hour after fine is paid. Bertram alone answers phone when we call in four days. Death to racist capitalism.

The black cassette was a recording. It was my voice saying the following:

"I'm in a place where there is no escape from. The group is serious, and they mean what they say. Janet, don't call the police. They don't want any deceit. They'll know if the money is marked, and they'll know if there are any bugs. I've told them about the family, and they have the names and addresses of everybody. Do what they say. They mean what they say. They don't want to be deceived. All I want to do is get out of here and get home, and they mean what they say, and Janet, talk to Buddy. They haven't harmed me, and I can't escape, so please do what they say. They know what they're doing, and they know what they want, so do what they say. Don't let the police influence you. Do what I say. Make sure the money isn't marked and that there are no bugs in the packages or anything like that. They will know if there is. Janet, don't be afraid to go with Buddy. The plan is a safe plan if you all cooperate. I am convinced they will either keep their word and let me go, or they will kill me. I'm banking on your cooperation. I'm anxious to be home with you and the children."

* * *

AT DAYBREAK THE FBI MOVED JANET and the boys to our friends' Barry and Joan's house. Janet never asked why. She grabbed Marc and Michael and left our home. She was terrified. She thought the kidnappers had been watching her and were going to kill me because she called the police. Looking back, the FBI was probably carving out space within the investigation away from the Nassau County police, especially given the discovery of the ransom letter and cassette tape.

Buddy was told to meet them at the house. Both he and Janet were given earpieces and two-way communication devices capable of facilitating conversation with the FBI at any time. There were no cell phones in those days. If Janet or Buddy encountered something suspicious or if something were to happen, they were to speak into the devices immediately. Their conversations would be recorded and help further the investigation. The officers came with black shoulder bags and microphones, but for some reason, they only tested Buddy's mic.

When they returned to my house, a female FBI agent named Margot Dennedy pulled Janet aside and showed her how the device worked, including how to change the battery. Dennedy was no ordinary FBI agent. She would go on to become the first female supervisor in the history of the Bureau, and more importantly to us, a lifelong friend and adopted family member.

Things continued to unravel at home. Janet tried to keep up appearances. She was instructed to act outwardly as if nothing were out of the ordinary, an impossible task. It was important for her to carry on some semblance of a normal routine. The police and FBI had to silo facts while the kidnapping was still developing. Tipping off neighbors, school teachers, the press, or whomever would put me in danger. Only later when the police felt it was time to make an official announcement could she make a plea to the public for help—assuming the kidnappers weren't caught first. Tipping them off that the police and FBI were on the case might force them to cut their losses. That wouldn't bode well for me.

Our son, Marc, was in first grade. He couldn't comprehend a kidnapping; no child should be put in that position. All he knew was his Daddy was gone, and he wanted him back. He also wanted to know who all of these strangers were in his house, and he wanted them gone.

"I want them to leave!" he told Janet. It was too much.

"Honey, these men are looking for a house in our neighborhood, and they don't live nearby," she said. "Daddy is away for work, and he got sick and can't come home right now."

It killed her to lie to Marc. It was yet another layer of the violation committed against our family. Victims don't just suffer a large singular abuse, but many abuses touching several lives that last in perpetuity. Janet hated lying. It's how she was raised and was a big part of how we tried to raise our children. We tell the truth in our family. But there she was, lying to him. She had to.

Marc still didn't understand. He wanted these people to leave and for our family to go back to the way it was. Me too, Marc. Me too. It enrages me that my captors could reach that far into my life and harm the heart of a child—my child. But that's exactly what they did.

Janet called my sister-in-law, Lois, Buddy's wife. She came and took Marc to their home in Larchmont, New York. Michael, our two-year-old, stayed with Janet one more night before her parents came and took him away. I don't know how Janet managed not to fall apart. To hear her tell it, her obsession became focusing on getting me back.

* * *

BACK AT THE TENEMENT, I was being "rewarded" for good behavior.

"You've been a good boy, Jack," the Keeper said. "You're being promoted."

He addressed the chains constricting my body. First, he disconnected my neck from the closet wall, then my feet. It had been three days and three nights in the closet. My reward? A metal-frame bed with a thin, musty mattress a few feet away. It was a meager upgrade.

But as soon as I was moved to the bed, my chains returned. My legs, still bound and padlocked together, were now fastened to the bed frame. My hands remained cuffed. The chain-link noose from the closet was gone, for now. It would be reintroduced nightly, with my neck padlocked to the head of the bed frame.

The Keeper unwound the adhesive bandage from around my head. Finally, after several days, I could see again—or so I hoped. But I couldn't see anything. It was dark. I squinted anyway. I assumed the Keeper donned his ski mask. I could feel him working the bandage with gloves on. I avoided his eyes, for his benefit and my safety, not knowing how he could see in there.

As the days wore on, I told him several times I didn't want to see him.

"Look, I don't want to see you. I don't want to know who you are. I don't want to see your face. I don't want to know anything. I just want to go home," I said.

I would turn away when he or they would come into the room. It was actually a ray of hope. They were so careful not to be seen and identified, and I was more careful not to look. I was lowering the cost, I thought, of them setting me free.

I wasn't sure what to make of it, but I'd been given a bed and the ability to move a little bit during the day. The Keeper put dark glasses over my eyes with tape stuck over the lenses and around the sides. I was left alone for longer periods of time.

He'd come and go. I assumed it was the Keeper, though I knew there was at least one other man involved—the near-silent driver with the shotgun from my driveway. I had no grasp on their plans apart from what I was told to say on the ransom tape. I had no concept of their movements. Whether they were in the next room or long gone, I had no way of knowing.

I worked up enough courage to remove the taped-over glasses from my eyes. It seemed like a death wish, like I was playing with fire. The action came long after the thought to do so. I became more comfortable, although far from it in any normal sense. Sometimes I'd wear the glasses, sometimes I wouldn't. Still, it was always black as night in the room. At times a rare sliver of light seeped in, whether from under the door or some other faint source. And when that happened, my eyes darted around the room soaking up details.

I saw a window boarded from the inside and a pipe next to it, probably a heating pipe. The ceiling was a lighter color than the darker walls. The room was small, about eight feet by eight feet, with a dark linoleum floor, one electrical outlet, a ceiling light that was never used, and the closet. That hideous, horrible space protruded maybe two feet from the adjacent wall and ran about five, maybe five and one-half feet long. It seemed like there should've been sliding doors, but there were none. The door to the room opened inward, and there were several locks outside of it. I was warned that the dark glasses better be on whenever the door opened. I hurried to put them on as soon as I heard the fiddling and clicking of the locks prior to their entry.

"You've been a good boy, Jack," the Keeper complemented another time.

A second "reward" was now granted: light. Not sunlight, of course, but a Sterno can—an ominous glowing, bluish flame, as if the flame carried the sinister afterglow of the Keeper's intentions.

We talked more as the days went on. He was bright. Sick, but bright. He was organized. Meticulous. Disciplined. Depraved. He thought through everything he said and did. He knew what he wanted. At one point, he told me he had a doctorate degree. He also said he had nine children. In the next breath, he said the plan was to kill me, but he talked his superiors out of it. He never mentioned who they were, and I wasn't entirely convinced they existed.

"This is going to teach you and your people not to keep all the money for yourselves," he said. "From now on, we're going to take what we want, when we want it. You know why? We have no fear of jail. We're not afraid like you."

"How many tenement buildings do you own? You see, we have to live in these buildings."

He said several times that we needed to pay him as soon as possible so he could help poor people and travel south to warmer weather.

"Your money is going out of the country. It's going to feed hungry poor people in other lands. It's going to help the Palestinians and poor black people," he said.

"We're not gonna let your people do to us what the Nazis did to you. We're gonna take what we want," he ranted.

* * *

ON THE EVENING OF MY PROMOTION, I was ordered to make another tape recording. Just like the first one, I was told what to say and how to say it. Again, the imperative was to be convincing. If by the Keeper's judgement I failed, it was over. It was all over. "You'll never see your family again," he said. His words grabbed and shook me to attention. I believed him.

I did as I was told the best I could. The theme was for Janet to deliver the money. I had to assure her that the kidnappers had a good plan. She had to trust them. She had to go. We rehearsed it again and again. It didn't have to be so hard, but it was. He wanted the recording done his way. I clasped the microphone. He would stop the recording and tell me it wasn't convincing. We'd start again. He gave me the tape recorder this time. "Turn it on. Turn it on. Turn. It. On. Not like that. Do it again," he'd say. I felt his frustration. I practiced what to say, then pressed the switch on the mic, toggling back and forth, on and off. My hands trembled under the pressure. I wasn't well.

After the tape, he wanted a picture. I was propped up on the bed, my back against a wall. I caught a glimpse of a long gray overcoat from the thin space beneath the rim of the taped-over lenses of my glasses. It was a different person, too tall and slim to be the Keeper. There had to be two people in the room. Two men. Was that three in total? Or more?

They put a blanket over my legs to hide the chains. It stank. It was filthy. It smelled sour, as if it'd been dampened by something foul and left untended to dry in some corner of this God-forsaken hovel. I still wore the same clothes from Tuesday night. I felt nauseous. They handed me a newspaper. The Keeper told me to hold it up for the picture. "Don't cover your face," he said. The picture would prove to my family that I was alive; the paper marked the date.

The Coffee Cup

I dreaded the nights. Then again, it always felt like night because the room was perpetually dark. Only a small hairline crack in the wood covering the window betrayed any sense of daylight. You could just make out a thin golden thread in those early autumn mornings. When it came, it felt like a special gift—a welcome if momentary reprieve from my thoughts and angst.

The isolation and solitary confinement were the extreme opposite of the rapid fire interrogations and anti-Semitic ramblings from the Keeper. I wasn't sure which was worse. During those long dark periods, the mind has nowhere else to go but inward, and that's not always the best place to be.

There were many moments during my captivity when I felt like I was being sucked into a giant dark hole—a long, huge tunnel. It was metaphysical. Maybe a dream, maybe not. I would lay chained on the closet floor or chained to the metal-frame bed and be transported horizontally into the tunnel. It was as if I were being pulled in by some unstoppable gravitational force. The only thing I could do was to accept my powerlessness. I had no idea what was happening to me. Was I cracking up?

Later, I learned it's a common phenomenon for people who've had close brushes with death. All over the world people have reported feeling as though they're being sucked into a long hallway or tube, or in my case, a tunnel. It shook me to my core. I was getting pulled into my own death, over and over again. It's truly a miracle I survived, and even more so with my mind relatively intact.

A big part of that was focusing my mind on my sweet and beautiful wife. If I didn't make it out of this mess, I hoped she would be able to say at my funeral that I was honest, a great father, and a caring husband. That made me content in my circumstances. I cared for her so much. I cared for her family; I had married them, too.

Then my emotions would swing like a pendulum to anger at my abductors. Those bastards made me convince my beloved wife to deliver the money! I took it for granted that they wouldn't hold up their end of their proposed deal. "Deliver the money, and Jack goes free. Deliver the money, and nobody gets hurt." *Fat chance.* The Keeper had already lied to me. He had said he'd let me go after they robbed me. And here I am, chained and tormented. Would they treat Janet the same way? Is she responsible for the Keeper's insane grievances, too? I never expected her to deliver the ransom—nobody would have. To want to do it is one thing, but to actually do it is another. The courage and the will she carried in her petite, innocent frame is something I'll never, ever forget.

Then the emotional pendulum would whoosh back in the other direction away from the torment the kidnappers inflicted on our family to tender thoughts of my children. Marc was six, Michael was two. My daughter was a glimmer on the horizon, not yet conceived. I thought of them many, many times during the loneliest hours. I felt their presence. I prayed ceaselessly that I would see them again.

My mind also jumped to escape, to freedom. I fixated on how I could break free. I tried and tried to get the handcuffs off. *If I could just loosen them a little bit, I could squeeze a hand through the hole*, I thought. I'd gladly trade some skin to strip a hand free. *And if I could just manage a hand, maybe I could free my legs, then I'd make a run for it. Yes!* I could feel the adrenaline when I fantasized about escaping. I would've done it. It might've worked. There were many times when nobody was around. I know because there were no sounds coming from the other room for hours at a time. Even during the day. No voices, no footsteps, nothing. But it was no use. The cuffs were too tight, and the chains were unbreakable. They were gone, doing whatever they were doing, and I wasn't going anywhere. I was in bondage with no escape.

My mind wandered back to the driveway. I'd get so mad at myself. I wasn't the fastest guy in the world, but maybe I could've lost the kidnappers in the woods behind my house. I replayed that scenario over and over again, visualizing the perfect moves like an athlete before an important game. I know the woods behind my house like the back of my hand; I'd lived in the area for 14 years. Plus, it was raining and dark. *Maybe they would have never caught me*, I thought. It burned in my gut, but I had chosen to go with them. And I'm glad I did, because Janet was inside with our two young boys.

Then I would try to flick off the thoughts like a switch. *What do these mind games matter, anyway? It's all so futile.* I'd cycle through these thoughts again and again only to conclude that there was no way out. I honestly thought I'd never get out of there. *Why would they take the risk of letting me go? What's the upside? If caught, they'd already go to prison for the rest of their adult lives. What's a few more years for murder that guaranteed I'd never talk to the police?* I kept thinking about the gasoline can in the car and the fumes on the Keeper's gloves. *At the end of the day, they're going to run off with the money and throw a lit match on this place on their way out. What did they have to lose?*

* * *

THE KEEPER ENTERED THE ROOM WITH A SURPRISE. "I'm going away for a bit. Maybe three hours, and I might get stuck in traffic," he said. "If you need anything, like food or a cigarette, tell him."

It was a new captor, a guard that came with special instructions.

"He doesn't speak English," the Keeper said. There was some whispering between them, but I couldn't make out any words.

"If you need to talk to him, you have to speak French," he said.

"I don't know French," I said.

The Keeper spent a few minutes teaching me the basics.

"When he comes in, you greet him. You say, 'Jambo.' Understand?" he said.

"Yes."

"If you need food, it's 'manget.' If you want a cigarette, say 'fire.' If he talks to you, and you don't understand, you say 'Umfudisi.' Understand?" he continued.

"Umfudisi. Yes."

"Oh, and you don't want to get smart with him. He's high strung, and he already doesn't like you. You know why?"

"Why?" I said, hesitantly.

"Because the Israeli Air Force bombed, napalmed, the village his wife and children were in. They killed them. Burned them alive. Imagine what he thinks about you."

He let his comment linger as if expecting me to answer. It was one of his sadistic rhetorical traps. "Imagine what he thinks about you." If I responded, the Keeper would've jumped all over me for talking back. "You don't tell me! I tell you!" I couldn't win. He enjoyed those moments. They reinforced his power. I laid there, unresponsive, muzzled by fear. I tried to sneak a slow inhale hoping he wouldn't take offense. It was all I could manage. I had no idea what to do. I didn't know if what he said was even true or not. He never mentioned the name of the stranger's Middle Eastern village or any other details, but it didn't matter. He had his desired effect. And with that, he left.

The new man left with him but stayed behind in the adjacent room. I could hear him on the other side of the door. He would stomp around and talk on the phone; that was part of his routine. It never seemed to ring, but at times I could hear him dialing out. He definitely spoke a foreign language, and I'm sure some of the calls were with the Keeper. I got the impression the new guy was slow-thinking and not very bright, not compared to the Keeper. I began to refer to him outright as Umfudisi. I got the feeling the Keeper would call him from time to time to check in and make sure he was doing what he was supposed to do: keep me alive and blind.

During the week of my captivity, there were perhaps three or four occasions when the Keeper informed me he was leaving the premises and that Umfudisi was in charge. All of these instances occurred after I was "promoted" to the bed, and they took place sporadically between long periods of isolation. The first time Umfudisi entered my room alone, I quickly acknowledged him with an obedient, "Jambo." It was my way of saying "hi," and "I'm no threat to you." He didn't respond. He just loitered for a while and said nothing. I could feel his menacing presence and wondered what he might do to me.

On another occasion I caught a glimpse of him walking out. He left the door open and a light on in the other room. The Keeper would've raged if he knew. I peaked at Umfudisi from beneath the frame of the taped glasses. He was tall, not what I expected. I figured he'd be heavy and of medium height, but he was very tall and thin. I only saw the back of him, but I noticed he had a limp. That was the reason for his heavy gait. That's why it sounded like he was stomping all the time. He dragged one leg and caught his full weight with the other. *Shhh-POOH, shhh-POOH, shhh-POOH.* The stomp was accentuated by the cheap, hollow construction of the tenement floor.

Umfudisi only spoke a few words the entire time. I'll never forget one of our final encounters. He freed one of my hands. It was exhilarating. I pulsed my fingers open and closed. I soothed my wrist with a gentle rub. My arms were no longer clasped together. It was so uplifting. He left the room, and I stretched my arms outward for the first time in days. The neck chains had been removed earlier that morning, and I felt free, save for my legs. I sat up and moved around more than I previously could on the bed. I felt liberated—which was kind of silly, considering.

But I had gotten too comfortable. Perhaps the mattress crinkled in a new way, or maybe the chains clinked oddly, because without warning the door burst open, and the Keeper jammed a pistol into my ribs.

"You trying to escape!" he yelled. Once again, he had his desired effect. My short-lived feeling of enjoyment was over.

* * *

I NEVER ATE ANYTHING IN THE CLOSET—nothing for three days. I wasn't going to give them the satisfaction, I thought. I was too terrified to eat, anyway. By the time I reached the bed, food was no longer something I could turn away. My first meal was chocolate—one of those big, thick chocolate bars. They put it in a plastic bag and told me to keep it. "Eat it when you're hungry and put it back in the bag when you're done. We don't want roaches in here," the Keeper said.

Once I started eating, he brought more food. Crackers made for my next meal, the thin square kind. Then peanut butter. Small bananas. Orange juice. A can of Mott's apple juice. A can of Planters peanuts. Eventually, a McDonald's hamburger with French fries and a can of Rheingold beer.

One time the Keeper said he had a special treat for me: homemade carrot cake. (To this day I can't eat the stuff.) It had a thin layer of icing on top. "No thanks," I said, reluctantly.

"It's healthy," he insisted.

"I had some recently. My wife made it. I can't eat it," I said, hoping not to set him off.

"You must've bought it from the Muslim sect," he said. "That must've been from a Muslim sect," he said.

I had no earthly idea what he was talking about.

Another time, he gave me a bag of dates. He dropped them next to me on the bed as he tidied up. When he left, I noticed a chartreuse green price tag on the cellophane wrapping with "$1.10" and the word "grocery" above it. I don't know why, but it was comforting—something normal from the outside world. Later, he brought in a container of Bobby Brooks spring water with a white cap. A sticker on the cap read, "31¢." Another time, he brought me a hamburger in plain white paper. It tasted unbelievably good. The circumstances were all wrong, but I allowed myself to secretly enjoy it. It was hot, and I imagined it coming from one of New York's finest diners.

One morning, the Keeper came in, removed my neck chains, and announced he was going out to get breakfast. "I'm gonna bring you some potatoes and eggs," he said. And he did, along with some coffee. He also told me, "You're not going to need your ears to eat," before putting plastic headphones over my ears. It was strange, and he never said why, but the last thing I remember as he was putting them on my head was the sound of church bells ringing in the distance. *Sunday,* I thought. *It's Sunday.*

The eggs were scorching hot. So was the coffee, and the potatoes were abnormally warm. I sat up, still in my work clothes from last Tuesday night. As I lifted the lid on the coffee, deaf and near blind but for the Sterno, it hit me. The coffee cup! I snuck a peek. There on the rust-colored coffee cup were white letters over a brownish background that read: "The Horizon Restaurant, Bronx, New York." The letters were patterned in a downward facing half-moon, or a horizon shape. It had an address: "Bronx, New York." Given the temperature of the coffee and eggs, I thought perhaps The Horizon Restaurant might be nearby.

From that point forward, I paid close attention to whatever would further pinpoint the kidnappers' hideout. The next morning, which had to be Monday, November 18, I heard the grinding gears of garbage trucks, the abrupt *pshhhh* release of air breaks, and hydraulic compressions as garbage men loaded and unloaded trash cans.

God bless them, I thought. As a lifelong New Yorker, it was amazing how comforting mundane city noises could be. They came back the next morning and continued working for an unusually long period of time, maybe two hours. Was I near some kind of garbage depot?

I also heard children around the same time. *School children*, I thought. If they're walking to school, then maybe there's a school around here. *That's a useful landmark to know*, I thought. I could hear their chatter and giggles, and shouting and chasing. They were innocent, playful sounds.

Later in the afternoon, I heard a heavy piece of machinery, like a tractor or bulldozer, or something similar. It sounded like it was loading debris onto another truck. *A construction site?* The rumble of the engine was much different than that of the garbage trucks earlier in the day. I had been forced to give up sight and yet, all of a sudden, my sense of hearing felt heightened. It's amazing how much one sense can grow when another is taken away.

Several times I heard vehicles that seemed to be traveling at a high rate of speed and in constant motion in a clockwise direction. They sounded like souped-up hot rods. Were they racing? Was it the kidnappers? A couple of times the occupants got out and started jawing at each other. It sounded friendly for the Bronx, I guess. I racked my brain trying to make out some words, but it was no use.

There wasn't that much regular traffic in the area, but there was a train. Judging by the audible *ta-tunk ta-tunk ta-tunk* and the screeching and slamming of metal wheels against metal tracks, I figured it had to be an elevated train or subway line. They're common in the boroughs, and it couldn't have been more than a couple of blocks away. It felt like a eureka moment at first, but then not so much. *Was it the 4, 5, or 6 train? The B or D? Maybe the 6? Wait, what if it's the LIRR? The Metro North?* I tried to gauge how far apart the trains ran to determine whether it could be an express or local line. It didn't work.

I also heard what must've been firetrucks. Was a station nearby? The sirens and blare horns blasted at irregular hours. I used the boarded window as a 12:00 point of reference to try to identify the location of the elevated train and the fire engine sounds. They seemed to come from a 10:00 direction. I felt like this was all going to be important if I ever got out of here.

There was a dog in a nearby building. It would bark at odd hours and trigger other dogs in the area to start barking. Sometimes someone would yell out for quiet. Sometimes someone would yell back.

Once I thought I heard a woman's voice in the other room. *Does she know I'm chained up in here like an animal? If I screamed for help would she call the police, or was that signing my own death warrant?* The more I listened for her, the more confused I became. The woman's voice seemed to come from the next room, but then it sounded like it was coming from the apartment above—or maybe outside? My newfound confidence was slipping away. *Ok, so there's a woman living upstairs, but is this a different woman?* I listened intently and wondered if I was hearing someone's TV. It was hopeless.

* * *

AS THE KEEPER CONTINUED TO COME AND GO during those later days, I could feel rage beginning to bubble inside me. First it was shock and abject fear, then I'd learned to block out his hatred the best I could and sift his words for survival clues. Now it was rage. I was so angry at him, but I was also so intimidated that it paralyzed me when he was around. I couldn't speak, and it was too dangerous to talk back even if I could.

There's a natural instinct in all of us to get angry when someone degrades your heritage or religious faith. It strikes at your core. It's universally wrong. It's unjustifiable to hurt someone because of how they worship, or for their conception of God, or for who their family is, or where they come from. I've never understood how people can do this. I wasn't raised that way. We were proud New Yorkers who loved our neighbors in the great melting pot that is our city.

But I couldn't fight back. Not in those circumstances. There was no debating. No arguing. No discussing. I had to let him rant at me in his most vile ways and swallow the humiliation. I couldn't afford for the Keeper to get upset, but my rage was brewing.

The theme of the Keeper's abuse was always that rich Jews were subjugating poor blacks and the Palestinians. I would've liked nothing more than to explain why that perception was so misguided—and so hurtful. None of it even involved me. I could've said a million different things on that account, but there was no opportunity. I was just expected to absorb his hate.

"The Jews take advantage of poor people," he said, over and over again. He didn't preach so much as lecture. He was always lecturing.

"The plight of poor people in America, Africa, and the Middle East is because of the Jews and the whites," he would pontificate. "The Jews are the world's slumlords. How many slums do you own?"

He thought nothing of how bigoted and offensive his words were. It didn't bother him in the slightest. I've met so many good people from different walks of life. What he was saying totally contradicted my experiences. Generalizing people as either good or bad based on their racial, ethnic, or religious backgrounds is something that I've always detested. It's wrong. Period. Full stop. *Not falling victim to his bigoted pathologies is going to be another win if I ever get out of here*, I thought.

He would say horrible, and I mean horrible, things to me about how the Jews were treated by the Germans. He would then tell me that the Jews were the Nazis to poor black and brown people. At times it seemed his racial theories were part smoke and mirrors to justify his actions. He'd hear himself, and it wouldn't make sense, like a fanatic who doesn't quite believe everything he says but nevertheless tries to believe anyway.

"We're not going to allow it," he would say. "We're not going to allow it." That was his bottom line.

"A man isn't a man in the ghetto, you see. How's a black woman going to respect a black man when he can't provide for her? He's not getting that respect. He can't support her. He can't provide for her.

He can't give her medical care. He's not a man—not a whole man," he rambled.

I've never been unsympathetic to poor people. Far from it. But to the Keeper, I was responsible for the ills of society or even the world. *My name is Jack Teich. I work in Brooklyn. I live on Long Island. I love my family. They mean everything to me. None of this other stuff has anything to do with me!* I didn't dare tell him. Not then. But a day would come when I would tell him everything, and he wasn't going to like it, not one bit.

* * *

ON MONDAY NIGHT, THE KEEPER MADE HIS MOVE. At 9:15 p.m., he called Buddy's house in Larchmont. His plan had been to push my family hard early and then go silent for several days. It would give Buddy and Janet precious time to get the money and to worry about getting me back. A worried family is a motivated family, he thought. Now, it was time to collect.

"Hello?"

"Hello. Buddy please," he said.

"Uh, Buddy isn't here. May I take a message please?" It was Lois, Buddy's wife.

"What time will he be in?"

"I don't know. Who's calling please?" she asked, although she was already putting it together.

"I will call back—"

"No wait! I can tell you where he is," she said.

"Quickly."

"Yes, he's in, um, he's in Great Neck," she responded.

"Yes," he said.

"You know the number?"

"Yes I do," he said, ending the call.

No sooner had he hung up than the phone rang back at my house on Kings Point.

"Hello?"

"Hello, Buddy?"

"Yes!" Buddy snapped to attention. He knew exactly who it was. Buddy and Janet had been waiting by the phone. The two previous calls had occurred at almost precisely the same time at night.

"Yes. Is my brother alive?" he asked.

"He is. He is alive, and he is well. Are you ready to make the exchange?"

"I have the money, but I must have proof that he is alive. I have the money," Buddy said.

"I sent you proof. You have it," the Keeper replied.

"You sent me proof? When?" Buddy asked.

"I sent the proof to you."

"The other night?" said Buddy.

"You will have—"

"Look. You can have the money. I've got three-quarters of a million dollars right here, but I want my brother."

"You will have him," said the Keeper. He was getting annoyed.

"You must prove this to me," said Buddy, holding firm.

"Now you listen to me carefully," the Keeper said.

"I'm sorry. What did you say?

"Tomorrow, be at Times Square, at the Information Booth, in front of the Times Building. That's all you need to know," the kidnapper said.

"Times Square Info Booth?"

"Be there at 6:30. Be at the telephone booth behind the Times Information Booth," he said.

"Wait one second," said Buddy. "Now is that 6:30 in the morning or in the evening?"

"Evening. Understand? I will call you at the phone booth behind the New York Information Booth at 6:30."

"Behind the New York Information Booth. Will you prove to me then that Jack is alive? When will I have proof he is alive? I will have the money with me. Three-quarters of a million dollars. It's every-thing I've got," said Buddy.

"Do you have the bag?" The Keeper was referring to the black satchel he put in the garbage bag at the Exxon station.

"I have it. I have the money in the bag you sent me. I've done everything that you have wanted."

"We will prove to you he is alive," said the Keeper.

"Before you get the money I want proof," said Buddy. But there was no response this time.

"Before you get the money," Buddy started again, but by then he was talking to a dial tone.

5

The Money Drop

On the morning of Tuesday, November 19, the Keeper charged into my room. "Wake up. We're taking your picture," he said. I was already awake. He unlatched the chains that secured my neck to the head of the bed frame, then removed my handcuffs. Similar to the first photograph, I was propped upright in the center of the bed. Once again, a stale musty blanket was placed over my lower body to hide my leg chains. "Take this," he said, as he gripped my wrist and forced the folded side of a crisp, unread newspaper into my hand. I felt the smooth texture of his glove.

The Keeper's aim was clear. He was proving to someone I was still alive.

He took away the taped-over glasses; it made no difference. The room was black just the same. "Look here and don't move," he said. I faced his voice. *Wham!* A single strobe of blinding light hit the room like an exploding star and was gone before my brain could fully register it. The camera shutter whirred and clicked. I rubbed my closed eyes. I hadn't seen light in close to a week. It burned. Still etched into my memory is the split-second image of my captor, ski mask on, illuminated, and standing over me before fading back to darkness.

The sting from the flash lasted the next few minutes as the Keeper locked my handcuffs again and put on my glasses before leaving. He returned a while later after developing the film. "Here, write on this," he said. He pointed a small handheld flashlight at my hands and gave me the photo and a pen. He told me exactly what to write: "Buddy, I'm okay. They will let me go. Today is one week. They have kept their word. I will call you tonight to pick me up. Please follow directions. You are not in danger. No police," I wrote, adding, "Love to Janet."

He told me to sign it, then he took it and left again.

They will let me go? I didn't know what to believe. I knew not to trust him, of course, but the prospect of freedom began eating away at my skepticism. I yearned to be home with my family. Since almost the very beginning, I resigned myself to doing whatever the Keeper told me, as it seemed the best way to survive. It was cruel to dangle that in front me when I was convinced they would kill me. The Keeper was careful to keep me ignorant of his plans. I never knew what would happen one moment to the next. Yet, I couldn't help but wonder: was tonight the ransom payment? Was tonight my last in captivity, or my last on Earth?

Time slowed to a crawl. I was now conditioned to the outside street sounds, and rescue fantasies had long since evaporated. I thought about my family and tried not to think about what the Keeper might do to me if he got his money. I waited for hours. Then, sometime later, the Keeper unlocked the door and poked his head in the room.

"I'm going out for a few hours. Someone will be here until I get back."

* * *

UNBEKNOWNST TO ME, MY FAMILY had successfully made $750,000 materialize out of thin air. I never knew the ransom amount until I was released—and I was floored. We had nowhere near that amount in liquid assets. Very few people would at that time, or today for that matter. Maybe a billionaire like John Paul Getty or the Hearst family, but the Teichs of Long Island? There was only one place where our family could hope to get that kind of money on such short notice: Acme Steel Partition and Acme Steel Door Corporation. Somehow, the Keeper knew it. I low-balled him about the company's finances as best I could during the interrogations, never once thinking he'd arrive at three-quarters of a million dollars.

Janet had little to do with the company. She certainly wasn't involved in its finances and banking arrangements. The FBI and Nassau County police mostly left her out of the emergency conversations and meetings with our banking partners. My brother, Buddy, wasn't included much either. Instead, they relied on Buddy Martin. He was Acme Steel Partition's accountant and financial advisor. He was also a family confidant and had been my brother Buddy's roommate in college. Buddy Martin had always been another brother to me, and when we most needed him, he rose to the occasion.

After an initial planning meeting at my home with both Buddys, the FBI, and NCPD detectives, Buddy Martin took over the process of securing the money to save my life. He coordinated the liquidation activities with Bankers Trust, Acme Steel's bank, and senior law enforcement officials. Thankfully, the company was profitable and of fair size. We employed 200 people at the time. My father, Joseph Teich, started Acme Steel in 1924, at the ripe age of twenty-two years old. With only a ninth grade education, he built a thriving manufacturing plant through grit, determination, and hard work. The company produced metal doors, frames, steel shelving, and partitions. My father started the whole thing from scratch.

Joe Teich was known as a tough but fair businessman. His sacrifices and success afforded a comfortable, suburban family life in Great Neck—where I chose to raise my own family. I went to high school there, ran track, and excelled at my schoolwork. I got an accounting degree at American University in Washington, D.C., and then joined the U.S. Coast Guard. Eventually, I returned to my father's company and earned the title of vice president by the time I was kidnapped. My job was primarily handling day-to-day operations on the manufacturing side of the business. Now, we were raiding it for money.

The company had both a pension fund and a profit sharing plan—which again, the Keeper knew about. The money in those funds belonged in large part to Acme Steel's employees. So the money existed, but we had to borrow it. It was a desperate financial maneuver that almost certainly wouldn't be allowed today. About two-thirds of the $750,000 came from those funds, which we took great care to later repay. It wasn't easy, especially considering the Internal Revenue Service tried to tax us for those disbursements. The other one-third of the ransom sum was taken from company bank accounts that paid for the normal costs of running the business.

Freeing up the money was one thing. Securing and preparing it for the money drop was another. Rigging the ransom package was, by itself, a monumental task conducted without the aid of modern technology.

As soon as Buddy Martin orchestrated the finances, the FBI descended on the vaults of Bankers Trust at its lower Manhattan headquarters. It took three efforts to get it right. First, the FBI proactively prepared a ransom payment in the amount of $250,000 in anticipation of an early payoff. Since there were no negotiations with the kidnappers, that amount was returned in exchange for the final demand of $750,000. But there was a problem. FBI agent Brian Corliss realized after the money had been bundled that the serial numbers in the 200 individual cash bundles—containing seven thousand $100 bills, two hundred $20 bills, and one thousand $10 bills—were arranged in sequential order, and they were brand new bills.

Tracking the money would be crucial to bring the kidnappers to justice. Giving them $750,000 in new, numerically ordered bills would have been like dealing an orderly deck of cards in a life-and-death game of poker. The jig would be up before the game even started. If the kidnappers felt tricked, they could cut and run. Any number of worst case scenarios could follow in addition to their escape, including killing me as the only witness to their crimes and perhaps harming other unsuspecting people down the road. The FBI had to get this right. That's when Buddy had a brilliant idea to "age" the money.

With time of the essence, Corliss ordered eighteen subordinate FBI agents to huddle in a conference room at the Bureau's midtown Manhattan field office. There, the agents hastily reopened the bundles of cash and painstakingly crumpled the bills to make them appear used. It was a tall order given the 8,200 freshly minted bills had been sitting in perfect piles inside a bank vault a short time earlier. The bills were crinkled into balls and straightened out, then passed between the agents to be folded and straightened again. The idea was to simulate normal wear and tear. Next, they shuffled and reshuffled the bills into disorderly piles of cash on the conference room table to break up the sequencing of serial numbers. Finally, they were shaped into equal stacks of matching dollar amounts for bundling.

The agents finished the process by randomly selecting a single bill from each new bundle and dusting it with a special forensic powder that could only be seen under fluorescent lighting. The bundles were then placed into a large manila envelope, as instructed by the kidnapping letter. The envelope was put into the black gym bag the kidnappers had planted in the trash can at the Exxon station near Buddy's house a few days before.

A convoy of FBI and New York City Police Department vehicles escorted Corliss, who was personally responsible for transporting the ransom, all the way from midtown to a heliport on Wall Street. There, a Nassau County Police Department helicopter waited to take him to the NCPD's Sixth Precinct in Manhasset, Long Island. From the Sixth Precinct police station, Corliss delivered the black gym bag to my house in Kings Point, where Janet and Buddy were preparing for the money drop back in Manhattan, not far from where the money had just come. But there was another glitch. FBI agents stationed at my home found that many of the accompanying photographs of the ransom bills' serial numbers were illegible. The photos would have to be taken again.

Amazingly, with Buddy Martin's help, the entire ransom was obtained and prepared in just two days.

* * *

DURING THAT TIME, FBI AGENT MARGOT DENNEDY was assigned to our home. She was on constant duty and essentially lived there. Besides being remarkably capable, Margot was a critical ally in helping Janet survive the ordeal. Janet had a petite frame and lost ten pounds that week. She couldn't eat. She couldn't sleep. Her nerves were shot, and her stomach was in knots. She had a terrible suspicion that the kidnappers would follow through on their threats to hurt her for going to the police. She was riddled with fear and haunted during the quiet hours of the night that they would kill her entire family, one by one. No one can endure that kind of stress without leaning on others for support. Janet needed help. Thankfully, Margot was there. She agreed to stay upstairs in Marc's room, which helped Janet endure the long, painful nights.

Janet was asked one last time if she was up for making the ransom payoff. She didn't flinch. "If I don't and something happens to Jack, I won't be able to live with myself," she said to a senior detective. Her bravery wasn't affirmed; it was met with a blank stare. Not long after, several agents and detectives whisked Buddy away for a planning session. Margot and Janet remained at the house. Without warning, Margot turned on Janet. Her behavior came out of left field. She was aggressive, mean. She started yelling at Janet and made wild, unfounded accusations. "You think this is all a joke, don't you?! Who do you think you are? Do you realize the trouble you've caused? Why don't you do everyone a favor and just quit?! Just get out of here!"

None of it made any sense. It was a complete personality change. Margot had been Janet's protector and confidant. She had shown Janet how to use the FBI communication device when the male agents ignored her, she had spent time with her, and she had shown Janet compassion. Now, Margot was lashing out with impunity. "Tell me why you're here! Tell me! What is it you want?! You need to grow up! Stop acting like a child!"

Something had gone terribly wrong. Margot berated Janet for being scared. She was cold and unfeeling. Janet tried to talk it out, but it was pointless. Margot was irrational. She spit sharp, unfair criticisms in rapid fire over Janet's objections. It was deeply hurtful. Janet became so confused and frightened by the mean-spirited mood swing that she ran upstairs to get away from Margot's vitriol. Janet was now completely alone. Her last shred of support had been ripped away. She locked herself in the upstairs bathroom.

Battered, exhausted, and psychologically traumatized, Janet later emerged from the bathroom when Buddy, the FBI agents, and police detectives returned. She could hear the low vibrations of their voices from the safety of the bathroom floor. She had reached a decision point. Janet could stay upstairs alone and removed from the ransom operation, or she could pull it together, march downstairs, and reintegrate into the group. She chose the latter. That's who Janet is. There was money to deliver, my life to save. And despite Margot's bizarre betrayal, Janet remained committed to the mission of getting me back. She was damaged but unbroken, wounded yet undeterred. Any lingering reservations had now been burned away. There was no backing out. Janet found her resolve.

When this became apparent, an FBI agent pulled her aside. "You passed the test, Janet. You're ready," he said. Margot had flipped on Janet to test whether she had the mettle to carry out the payoff. It was mean but necessary from their perspective. Janet was a civilian, a suburban housewife and mother of two young children. Yet she volunteered to cross paths with armed, anti-Semitic revolutionary militants carrying today's equivalent of $4 million in cash. She was going to walk into Times Square with that kind of money and danger to save my life. Margot had offered to make the payoff in Janet's place, but Janet feared the kidnappers would know that it wasn't her... that she had not followed their plan...and she would be killed. And I would be killed. She would not take that chance. Janet was determined to deliver the money, but the FBI and police detectives knew any number of things could go wrong. They understood from experience that no plan ever unfolds how it's supposed to. They needed to know that Janet had the inner strength to persist under intense pressure. If she had failed the test, Margot was prepared to take her place and assume all of those risks. Margot was a friend, indeed.

* * *

It was all coming into focus. The FBI and Nassau County police officials were crossing their final t's and dotting their last i's. Bureau agents, detectives, and uniformed cops from across the New York City metropolitan area were readying themselves for what had been officially dubbed, Operation Jacknap—a mashup of "Jack" and "kidnap." I'll never forget their service. Off duty law enforcement officers were turning up in droves and volunteering to participate. All of those brave men and women were committed to securing my safe return and to justice being served. I'm forever in their debt. There were hours of briefings leading up to the money drop. The smallest details were covered and drilled again and again. Every strategy was met with a counter strategy. Emergency scenarios were game planned and contingencies were constructed. Now, it was time to move.

Both Janet and Buddy were fitted with two-way radios supplied by the FBI. They were cutting edge technology at the time, enabling the sending and receiving of messages while moving about. By then, Janet and Buddy were well-practiced. As the kidnappers' letter instructed four days earlier, they climbed into Buddy's small BMW and headed for New York City. Janet placed the black gym bag at her feet. A caravan of FBI agents and Nassau County police officers and detectives followed behind. A surveillance helicopter whirled overhead. The whole scene was surreal.

The destination was Times Square, one of the most pedestrian traveled areas on Earth. They had to meet at a telephone bank at the Times Square Information Booth at precisely 6:30 p.m. The kidnappers were going to call a random pay phone and give further instructions, but Janet and Buddy had to get there first. The plan was to take the Long Island Expressway. Almost immediately, they ran into traffic.

"C'mon! Let's go," said Janet in frustration. It was rush hour in the nation's largest, most densely-packed city. The caravan left with plenty of time to make the rendezvous, but each passing minute in traffic made it feel like they'd miss the call. They could see the Chrysler and Empire State buildings ahead, as well as other Manhattan skyscrapers. "It's taking forever to get there. C'mon!" Buddy kept bouncing his leg and tapping his fingers on the seat. Janet closed her eyes and took long, slow breaths. Closer and closer they got. Janet tried to calm her nerves. They drove in relative silence.

Finally, they made it. There was no time to waste. Trudging through Times Square under normal circumstances is tricky, even for native New Yorkers. You never know what you'll encounter in the densely concentrated commercial cityscape. Stores, restaurants, playhouses, newsstands, pornography booths, and clusters of businessmen, sailors, tourists, prostitutes, and everything in between makes for an electric few blocks of real estate. Carrying $750,000 in cash through the mix made the experience radioactive.

Janet and Buddy knew the FBI and the police were watching them, but were the kidnappers? Janet donned a white scarf, just like they said. They weren't clear where she was supposed to wear it, but the idea was to be able to recognize her in a crowd. So she tied one white scarf around her neck and another to her handbag.

At almost exactly 6:30 p.m., a pay phone rang. Buddy took a deep breath and picked it up.

"Hello."

"Buddy?"

"Yes. We have the money. Are you here?" he asked.

"Go to two telephone booths outside the main U.S. Post Office on Eighth Avenue, across from Madison Square Garden," the voice said. "Wait for a call."

Buddy repeated the instructions. The caller hung up. He repeated the instructions for Janet and for the agents listening in through the two-way radios. "Let's go," she said.

As they began to walk, a staticky voice cut into their ear pieces. "*Shhh,* Go to the curb. *Shhh,* Act like you're hailing a cab. *Shhh,* A yellow taxi is going to pick you up. Get in."

Janet and Buddy walked along Broadway and waved for a cab. Just as the voice said, a yellow taxi pulled up. An undercover FBI agent posed as the driver. They got in without speaking to him. He knew exactly where to take them. It was important to keep radio-silent whenever possible to keep the channel free from distraction. That meant no talking unless absolutely necessary. In her nervous state, Janet accidentally broke protocol. When exiting the cab at the Post Office, she noticed the metered fare was ninety-six dollars. "Are we going to pay that?" she asked Buddy.

It was a human moment, reflective of her innocence and the fact that she and Buddy were never told about the FBI and police's plans. They didn't know how many agents and officers were involved, and they didn't know where they were. Similarly, the kidnappers kept them clueless from one moment to the next to throw off the police. As it happened, there were hundreds of law enforcement coalition members scattered about the area.

The brief car ride allowed Buddy to rest his arms. The black bag seemed to grow heavier along the way. They got out of the cab and approached the outside phone booths. Almost immediately one of the telephones rang. They were being watched.

"Go to Penn Station," the caller said. "Inside, there are telephone booths at Track 17 on the Long Island Railroad. Across from the booths is a bank of lockers. Go there now. Wait for my call."

Buddy repeated the caller's directions. The line went dead. "Did you get that?" he asked Janet, knowing the agents were listening in.

Evening had turned into night, but you couldn't tell inside Penn Station. It was a beehive of activity. An endless stream of travelers scurried in different directions hustling through the labyrinth of tunnels and platforms. There was a constant flow of people. Among them were the kidnappers and the cops. They both spied Janet and Buddy—and the ransom—as they moved through the crowds. Each time a new track announcement hit the station board and blared through the P.A. system, a standing crowd would rush to the appropriate track. Most of them just wanted to go home after a long day's work. The last thing Janet needed was to get knocked around in the stampede.

When they made it to Track 17 of the LIRR, Janet spotted the telephone booths. "Over there!" she pointed. They walked briskly together. Janet found a key in one of the booths. Next to it was my picture. It was the photograph the Keeper had taken earlier in the day. She held it in her hands. It sparked a mix of emotions: sadness, anger, fear, resolve. She flipped the photo over and instantly recognized my handwriting. "Buddy, I'm okay. They will let me go...Please follow directions...No police...Love to Janet."

The phone rang. Buddy picked it up.

"Tell Janet to go to Nedick's food stand and wait outside. Do it now," the voice said. Buddy relayed the message, and Janet left to find the food stand. It was about 150 feet away, maybe the longest 150 feet of her life. Her eyes darted from face to face in the passing crowds. Some made eye contact for a split second as they passed. She glanced at shady characters loitering throughout the underground maze. She was physically smaller than almost everyone in her path. *Is he one of the kidnappers? Maybe him, over there?* What were they going to do to her, she wondered.

Janet pursed her lips and tried to conceal her mouth as she spoke into the radio. "Can you see me? I'm standing in front of Nedick's food stand. Are you close by?...Hello?...Can you hear me?" There was no answer. "Hello? Are you there?"

At the same time, agents were attempting to contact her. Nothing. Just static. The radios didn't work underground. The agents and police officers struggled to communicate with each other, let alone with Janet and Buddy. She was petrified.

"Use the key to open the locker across the way," the kidnapper told Buddy back at the pay phone. "There's a number on it. Put the money inside and leave the key in the lock. Then go switch places with Janet. Tell her to come back to this telephone. Don't hang it up. Do as I say. GO," the voice said.

Buddy jumped into action. He toted the heavy bag over to the bank of lockers. But what seemed clear on the telephone a moment ago now seemed convoluted and unclear. In his confusion, Buddy put the ransom bag in the wrong locker. The kidnapper gave too many directions at once, and under the pressure, Buddy screwed up. Unaware, he fast-walked to find Janet and relieved her from her post.

"Go back to the telephone booth. It's off the hook. He wants to talk to you. Hurry," Buddy told her.

"The radios don't work," she whispered.

"There's no time right now," Buddy said. "The money's in the locker. You've gotta go."

Janet hurried back to the Track 17 phone booth and picked up the idle receiver. "Buddy can't be trusted," the voice said on the other end. "Go to the next phone booth, get the key, and go to the locker. Inside there's a bag. Take it. Then go get Buddy and go back to the Eighth Avenue telephone booth. A black Chrysler will come for the ransom."

Janet took a deep breath. It was a complicating wrinkle. She didn't feel safe, and the directions didn't seem to make much sense. But she put her head down and pressed on. Unknowingly, she was being directed to a different locker and to a decoy bag that looked

identical to the black gym bag containing the money. She ran over
and got Buddy, and the two of them went back to the Eighth Avenue
phone booth outside of the Post Office. They thought the payoff had
gone off without a hitch and half-expected me to magically appear.

They waited for a woman to finish using the pay phone they
needed. She was arguing and carrying on. Janet and Buddy were getting increasingly worried about how long she was taking, knowing
the kidnapper might've been blocked from getting through. Buddy
was about to give her a disapproving look while tapping his watch—
the universal signal to hurry up. That's when the woman shouted,
"I want the money." Buddy stopped and looked at Janet. Both were
frozen, wide-eyed. Was she with the kidnappers? But the woman
slammed the phone down and walked off muttering expletives to herself. Turns out it was nothing. Just a random New York City moment.

The phone rang almost immediately after. It was the kidnapper.
He was irate. "What are you trying to pull! You want to see Jack alive
or not?!"

"What?" said Buddy. "I don't understand. We gave you the
money!"

"Don't play games with me!" the kidnapper screamed. "I'm warning you. This is your only chance."

"Look, we gave you the money. I put it in the locker. The money
is in the locker just like you said. No tricks," said Buddy.

"You took the key! The money's locked in the locker!"

Buddy begged for a chance to make it right. But what neither
the kidnappers nor Buddy realized was that he had accidentally put
the moneybag in the locker directly above the one he was supposed
to use and left that key. All the yelling and confusion was over a few
inches of space separating where the $750,000 was and where it was
supposed to be. The money was just sitting there now, available for
anyone to take should they be lucky enough to stumble upon it.

"Go back and leave the key in the locker!" the kidnapper demanded.

Janet and Buddy ran as fast as they could to the bank of lockers
at Track 17, LIRR. They panicked when they got there. They couldn't

remember which one it was. There was a long wall of identical lockers, except some had keys and some didn't. Buddy ran to call the FBI for help from an adjacent battery of pay phones, but before he finished dialing the emergency contact number, Janet screamed, "Wait!"

She wasn't ready to quit. Still carrying the decoy bag, Janet bounced from locker to locker, trying to open every one she could reach. What about the money? By that time it had already been left unattended for almost half an hour. Janet ran back to the original phone booth across the plaza from the wall of lockers, retraced her steps, and tried to jog her memory. It worked.

"Found it!" she called to Buddy.

They opened the correct locker together. Inside was an empty blue gym bag similar to the black ransom bag. Then Buddy had his own flash realization. He'd put the money in the locker above. Janet reached for it, but it was too high and too heavy. Buddy grabbed the moneybag and put it in the right place. This time he left the damn key in the lock.

They ran back out of the station and over to the Eighth Avenue phone booth. They'd done their job, now it was time for the kidnappers to do theirs. They waited for the call. And waited. They lingered and were prepared to shoo away anyone who got close to the booth. *Why isn't he calling?* Fearing the worst, Buddy turned around and spoke covertly into the radio receiver with mixed results. "*Shhh,* Sit tight. *Shhh,* We've got you." After another thirty minutes, the phone rang. Buddy jumped for it.

"Hello."

"You did a good job...Jack will call. Go home."

It was over, for now. Relieved but unsatisfied, Janet and Buddy ambled to the steps of the Post Office building and sat down to rest. They waited for directions from the FBI, who were embroiled in their own fiasco.

Agents and officers positioned around Track 17 had witnessed a black male approach the ransom locker after Janet and Buddy had fled the area. He fiddled with its contents and removed a blue vinyl gym bag. The man had taken the manila envelope stuffed with the bundles of cash from the black bag and placed it in the blue bag. He wore a fedora-like hat and long coat down to his knees. As he glided through the station, a catastrophic breakdown in communication and visual contact ensued.

Operation Jacknap's prime objective was to secure my safe return. Second was recovering the money. The army of more than 450 agents, detectives, and police officers who flooded the area could do nothing to endanger my life. That meant following the ransom man instead of arresting him on the spot. Once I was safely released, then they'd make their move. But as the man moved from one sector of surveillance through another, he disappeared. The agents couldn't alert each other or risk tipping him off. The ransom man blended into the passing crowds, carrying the unfamiliar bag. He veered toward the Seventh Avenue side of Penn Station and descended down to a lower level subway platform. There, he walked right by an undercover police officer, got onto a subway train, and vanished.

6

The Jade East Motel

"Time to go," the Keeper said to me.

He launched into the room and unlatched the padlocks binding me to the metal-frame bed. It had been hours since he announced he was leaving, and in typical fashion he barged in without notice. As he jostled the chains around my legs, I couldn't help thinking about the photograph he made me write on earlier in the day. *They will let me go....* I didn't know if he got the ransom or not, but removing the chains for the first time meant we were going somewhere. The question was, where?

He sat me upright on the edge of the bed with handcuffs and taped glasses on. He began preparing our exit and tidied the room. Without much impetus, he said, "It's over," and that he was taking me to call Janet.

"Thank God," I said with a sigh.

He stopped. "What? What did you say?!"

I'd triggered the intimidation game. I braced for impact. "What. Did. You. Say?!!" he repeated louder. I didn't answer.

"No! You don't thank God. You thank the black righteous man!"

He was indignant. Had I learned nothing from him? He was in charge, not God. That was the message.

The Keeper then left the room and returned with a bag of supplies. I felt them drop beside me. He pushed my head back coldly. "Hold still and keep your eyes shut," he commanded, removing the darkened glasses. He started smearing thick liquid all over my face. It had a pungent, familiar smell. It was shoe polish. *Shoe polish?* Then he stuck two large Band-Aids over my eyes and put the dark glasses back on. "Get up," he said, grabbing my arm.

That whole evening I had heard banging in the other room. They were hammering nails into what sounded like a wooden box. *My coffin?* I heard them using what sounded like tinfoil. Unrolling strips, ripping them across a serrated edge on the box, then wrinkling and crumpling the strips into place.

The Keeper unlocked the handcuffs. "Don't be stupid," he warned. "Arms out." He slung my dingy suit jacket on me. Then he put the overcoat I'd worn a week earlier on me. It was a clumsy process. Then he guided me out of the room with one hand on the back of my neck, the other on my shoulder. I hadn't walked in a week. Blood rushed down my aching legs.

The Keeper marched me out of the one-room prison and into the next room. "Sit down," he said. He pushed me down while I tried to find the seat. It felt like another bed, except lower to the floor. The Keeper spoke a few words in a foreign language. I assumed he was talking to Umfudisi. Then he spoke in English.

"We thought about killing you," the Keeper said.

"We thought a lot about it. But I stuck my neck out for you. I convinced them that there are other ways to reach the same end. We don't have to kill you. That's why you're not permanently immobilized right now," he said. "What would that prove? It's more important for you to go back and teach others about poor people.

You need to tell your people not to keep all the money. You need to give that money to black charities. You need to teach your children right. And we're gonna check up on you. We know who you are. We know your names. We're gonna make sure you're giving your money to charity. You don't need all that money. This is a good lesson for you."

I didn't dare say a word. *Let him have his stupid moment,* I thought. Don't do anything to provoke his insanity. The Keeper claimed he was doing me a favor. And even though I deserved the ultimate punishment, he let me live as a testament to his wisdom and righteousness. He then gave me a shot of scotch. It was supposed to seal our understanding.

The Keeper grabbed my arm and jerked me upright. "Here, use this like a blind man," he said, handing me a long wooden broomstick. It was some kind of a makeshift cane. "Tap it. Let me see you tap it around," he said. I knew the routine. He wanted me to be convincing. My life depended on playing along.

We walked out of the tenement apartment, turned to the right, and went down some steps. Then a few more paces, a landing, and down several more steps. It was the reverse of how we came in a week earlier. The Keeper put a hat on my head before we stepped outside. He pulled it low. We walked together to a nearby car. He opened the door, grabbed my arm, and bore some of my weight as I got in. He pressed down on my head with his other hand, so as not to bang it on the roof. I grabbed the window for support. He put me in the front seat. I remembered the gasoline can. My gut flipped. Then the Keeper put wax in my ears, but he didn't do it very well, because I could still hear. With a turn of the key, he sparked the engine, put the car in gear, and we took off. *Where are we going? Was he lying again?*

It was just the two of us. He didn't say anything until about twenty minutes later when we stopped at a toll. I don't know if it was the same toll as before, but it was unmanned. I'm sure he planned it that way. The Keeper dropped a coin in the machine, but he dropped the other coin on the ground by mistake. "Keep your head down!

Don't move. Look at the floor." He was frazzled. He opened the door and looked around but couldn't find the coin. The last thing he wanted was to call attention to the car. It was almost 11 p.m. If the Keeper blocked the toll lane much longer, horns would start blaring. Blowing through the toll wasn't an option either; it could attract a cop. He started rummaging around looking for another quarter while growing increasingly upset. Was he going to lose $750,000 over twenty-five cents? I heard him open a zippered bag and fumble through it. He found a coin and made sure to drop it in the machine correctly. In his agitated state, the Keeper projected his anxieties onto me.

"You wanna know the reason why we took you?" he said. He turned from the road toward me as he spoke over the rev of the engine and past the jiggered ear plugs. "Because you have disregard for poor people."

"Now I tried to talk to you," he continued. "But you wouldn't listen to me. I tried to talk to you, but you were always busy, and you would never listen. I'm talking to you, Jack Teich of Acme Steel."

I didn't know where he was going with his rant. It made no sense. Just more angry rambling. Was he psyching himself up for a dramatic finish? The thought was chilling. He wasn't really talking to me so much as to himself. He spoke to me as if I were a symbol of all that was wrong in his warped worldview. Speaking to me meant speaking to everyone like me. Yet, he never even pronounced my name properly. He'd say, "Jack Tarsh."

"You, Jack Tarsh of Acme Steel, you would never listen. I tried to talk to you, but you would never listen to me. You were always too busy. But I'm not busy. I'm not busy now. I took time out for you, and I made you take some time away. You needed it. You had to take the time away," he said.

The Keeper then began to name every member of my family. My father, my brothers, my in-laws...everybody. He knew the names and ages of my children. He recited every phone number, address, vehicle, and birthday that we discussed during my closet interrogations. He knew odd facts and minor tidbits, and he wanted me to know that he wasn't reading the information. He'd committed it all to memory.

"You know I'm not reading this because I'm driving the car. Your information is all up here," he said, a reference to his psychotic brain. "If anything ever comes out that only you would know—something we talked about, something that happened, anything that could only come from your mouth—then you know I can find you. And you know, I know what to do."

He didn't say what he'd do, but the intimation was that he'd kill me, or someone close to me, as a punishment for talking. He told me several more times over the next twenty to twenty-five minutes that he hoped I'd learned from my abduction. We slowed down. He pulled off on what must have been a side street and drove at an idle speed for a minute or two before making a U-turn. Then he stopped the car.

"When you get out of the car, turn to the right. Walk ten steps and you'll be next to a phone booth. Count to fifty. Then call Buddy. He'll be at your house. I told him that you would be dropped off," he said.

I pawed the air for the door handle. "Wait!" he said before I opened it. "It's later than I told Buddy. So if he called the authorities, then you tell him to call them back and tell them to forget about it. That everything is fine. Understand?" he said.

"Yes," I replied.

"Now get out."

As I climbed out I thought of his shiny pistol from my driveway. "One, two, three…" I counted, half-expecting a bullet to the back of my head. But it never came. The car began pulling away, the engine noise getting quieter and quieter. I waited until I couldn't hear it anymore, then took off the darkened glasses and coverings from my eyes. *Where am I?* I threw off the hat and dropped the makeshift cane. There was no phone booth. He lied. But he was gone. And I was alive.

With shoe polish slathered on my face, I surveyed the foreign ter-rain. Not sure where to go, I walked to a nearby gas station for help. It was empty. I was alone and frantic, an easy target. Fast-walking along the street, I came upon a building with parked cars all around. The Jade East Motel.

Stumbling inside, I spotted a phone near the lobby entrance. My fingers trembled as I tried to dial the number to my house. My breathing was rapid and heaving. The phone rang several times. Janet finally answered the phone, surrounded by law enforcement.

"Janet, it's Jack. I'm alive. I'm at the Jade East Motel. Get here as fast as you can! Tell Buddy he dropped me off late. Tell him—"

"Jack! It's ok," she interrupted. "It's ok. It's all taken care of. Just stay there. Don't leave."

The FBI was able to trace the number, and agents were already on the way. The Jade East Motel was on Conduit Avenue, a service road off the Belt Parkway near John F. Kennedy International Airport. I exited the front entrance to the street and stood waiting. Within minutes a car approached. Three men were inside.

"Jack?" the driver asked from his open window.

"Yes."

"FBI. You're all right. You're safe now."

It took a second for those words to register. But when they seeped in, they hit hard. A spasm of short breaths bubbled up from within my chest, and I broke down and wept. I was going home.

* * *

IT WAS AROUND 11:40 P.M. I was safely inside Agent John Westhoff's unmarked car as more than two dozen FBI and police vehicles carrying more than sixty agents and detectives descended on the motel. They proceeded in a coordinated fashion, as if the kidnappers might still be there. It was an impressive display.

Agent Westhoff later described the experience as having picked up a "disheveled, dirty man" outside an airport motel. He and at least one other team were assigned to patrol the Kennedy Airport area and were in the vicinity of the motel at the time of my release. It was heartbreaking to know how close they came to the Keeper himself and that he slipped past them. Others almost certainly passed the Keeper going the opposite direction on the way to the Jade East.

It was naïve to think they would take me straight home. Instead, I was whisked away to the FBI's midtown Manhattan headquarters for a lengthy debriefing. Janet was simultaneously en route from Kings Point.

I arrived exhausted, unshaven, filthy, and too distraught to speak. I was shrouded in the same brown suit—now soiled—I wore the morning I went to work one week ago, unaware of the fate that would befall me. I will never forget entering the FBI headquarters—another moment frozen in my mind. As I shuffled my bedraggled body into the giant room filled with gray government desks, the entire room and scores of FBI agents and employees all stopped, stood up, and stared at me, as if someone had hit a pause button. Two agents, one on each arm, propped me up as we bee-lined to Assistant Director John Malone's office on the other side of the building.

A doctor performed a thorough physical. He asked if I'd been drugged. I don't know if that was routine or because I was so despondent. "Did they inject you with anything? Any pills? Any unusual substances? What about in your food? Do you have any medical conditions?" the doctor asked.

Then the law enforcement questioning began. "What happened, Jack? Start from the beginning. How many were there? Get any names? Tell us about them. What did they want? Why you, Jack? Did they say why they picked you? What can you tell us about where they're going? Tell us everything, Jack. We want every detail."

They pushed and pushed. I felt so debilitated. I couldn't talk. I couldn't get the ball rolling. I was too tired. It was all too fresh, and I was too scared. Sure, I was safe there, but what about in a month? Or in a year when they'd all forget about me? They kept pushing until I mustered enough energy to say, "Unless you assure me that my family is safe, I have no interest in talking."

I needed their buy-in. They wanted the kidnappers. Good. But are we still in this together or not? I looked at Edward Curran. He was Chief of Detectives for the Nassau County Police Department. With him was Chief Inspector Owens and Deputy Inspector Danny Guido, both of the NCPD. Guido would prove to be the brightest law enforcement mind I'd ever encountered. FBI agent Fred Behrends was the interviewer. He did most of the questioning while the others listened and scribbled notes.

"I'm not talking unless you can assure me my family will be safe," I said. "I have too much at stake."

Curran conferred with Owens and Guido for a moment. Then he said, "Jack, I assure you. Your family will be protected."

They gave me their word. I trusted them. And they kept their word.

After thirty minutes of struggling to relive the week-long nightmare, one hellish detail at a time, there was a knock at the door. An aide peered in. "Jack, someone is here to see you." The law men looked at each other, got up, and left. In came my beautiful, precious Janet. As soon as I laid eyes on her, my body went limp. Tears overtook me. She wept as we embraced as one. We made it. We survived. She smelled like love and home. Her hair was sweet and smooth. She wore green slacks and a flowered blouse. Our eyes met and spoke the words we couldn't say. I marveled at how this petite, thirty-year-old woman who mothered my children could willingly thrust herself into the jaws of evil to save me. She brought me a sandwich with a cold beer and a complete change of clothes. "Why did you take so long to answer the phone when I called?" I asked. I didn't know what else to say. Janet smiled and answered so sweetly, "So they could trace the call for us to find you and get you home."

When we were ready, I called for the questioners to return. I was breathing much easier. The catharsis in Janet's arms was everything I needed to continue.

Another thirty minutes passed before the next interruption. Buddy had arrived. It was good to see him. "Thank you, Buddy." The FBI steered him and Janet into a separate room, eager to debrief them about the ransom payment they delivered earlier Tuesday night. It was now two hours into Wednesday morning, November 20.

The press had arrived. John Malone, assistant director of the FBI and head of the New York field office, convened a news conference slightly past 2 a.m. The media knew about the case and had been waiting patiently for days. My abduction was an enormous story. It had all the elements of a stirring news saga that could reach into the homes of millions of New Yorkers and deliver headlines for years to come. The media was hungry and wanted to be fed.

Malone, flanked by Curran, told reporters that a $750,000 ransom had been paid to my kidnappers at 8:30 p.m. and that I was released at 11:20 p.m. near JFK airport. Malone announced that I was in "pretty good shape" and had not been "grossly mistreated" despite being chained in a closet and to a bed for a week. He relayed that I had undergone a medical evaluation and would not be transported to a hospital at that time. In an effort to alleviate the potential for the juiciest part of the event from spinning out of control, Curran added that there was no evidence that the kidnapping had "political overtones," but he also stated that their investigation was not ruling out the possibility at that time. Additionally, he said the kidnappers were still at large.

"Our job is half done. We have the victim home safely," Curran said.

The kidnapping especially resonated within our Long Island community. Not just because we lived there, but because that's where the story broke—although the intrepid journalist never received his full glory. Gene Batzer of the *Long Island Press* had learned of my kidnapping about twenty-four hours after it happened. Rather than break the biggest story ever to hit Great Neck, he chose to sit on the scoop of his career to protect me and my family.

The first ransom call had just transpired, and Batzer was at the Nassau County police headquarters in Mineola working on another story. Six members of a single family had been shot in Amityville, and all hell was breaking lose at the station. While working his police sources for information, an officer said something off-the-record about another tragedy. "A kidnapping," the officer said. "Kidnapping?" That's all he said. It was too dangerous for the victim to say anything more at that time, he explained. A half-dozen phone calls later, however, and Batzer put it together: a North Shore steel executive had been abducted from his home and held for ransom.

But instead of rushing to print and cashing in, Batzer and his editors called Chief Curran to say that the *Press* would not publish "the Teich abduction" exclusive if it would put me and my family at risk. Curran was skeptical. He'd been burned in the past. In 1956, a four-week-old baby boy named Peter Weinberger had been abducted from a carriage on the front steps of the Weinberger home. The child's decomposed body was later found in some weeds beside a road. The police never had a chance to help negotiate Weinberger's release, and some in the law enforcement community speculated that the media uproar spooked the baby's kidnapper. A man named Angelo Lamarca, thirty-one, was eventually arrested. He confessed and was executed in 1957.

Batzer and the *Press* adhered to the agreement—to the determent of the paper's notoriety and sales—with Curran offering to keep them in the loop. As other metropolitan area newspapers, television networks, and radio stations caught on, the police, with the endorsement of the FBI, promised to alert them of any breaks in the case as well if they would remain silent until I was freed—or dead. All but one Manhattan-based tabloid cooperated. Janet had not only requested to keep the story quiet, but out of an abundance of caution she asked the FBI and NCPD to wait until I was released before pursuing the kidnappers. It was Bureau policy to apprise a victim's family of these options in a kidnapping situation and then to follow their wishes.

Janet was first to emerge from the interview sessions. Mine continued until 4:50 a.m. It was time to go. She left shaken to the core. The questioning had the effect of conveying how dangerous the ransom payment had been and how vulnerable she was. It was also made clear that the kidnappers had gotten away, and our family was still at risk.

Buffered by FBI agents and police detectives, we faced a gaggle of determined reporters and cameramen all shouting and jockeying for position. "How do you feel, Jack? Tell us about the kidnappers!" "Why'd they pick you, Jack?" "How does it feel to be free?" "Can you comment?" I've got nothing against the media. They were doing their jobs. But it's oppressive for people who don't want the attention. As we were escorted through the gauntlet, Curran whispered something to Janet and pointed. She stopped. Our bodyguards allowed an opening as she approached an individual reporter with an extended hand. It was Gene Batzer.

"We'd never have him back if it weren't for your help and the help of these outstanding men," she said, fighting back tears. He nodded and asked for an interview. She politely declined. "I still have my family to think of."

Days later, Batzer would write of the experience: "For the first time in my life I knew that I held the fate of a man's life in my hands... A journalism professor had always told me to be responsible. He said it was the most important thing for a reporter to be. Freedom of the press is guaranteed by the Constitution, but possibly endangering a man's life for expression of that freedom at this moment seemed ludicrous.... The days of frustration experienced in holding back the story came out on the typewriter, and I breathed easier. And most importantly, a man's life had been saved."

I peered through the crowd and approached Batzer myself.

"I want to thank you for your humanity and your cooperation in holding back the release of the story. The kidnappers had their ears to the radio."

It was true. The Keeper was very surprised at the lack of news coverage. He thought the media wasn't saying anything to protect my elderly father. "He might've collapsed at hearing the news," he said.

News articles with two-inch headlines hit every major paper across the greater New York City area that morning. A particular photo of Janet circulated across the spectrum. She looked terribly unhappy, although she was elated that we were together again. Janet believed the kidnappers were going to kill her during the payoff. They threatened to kill everyone in our family if she went to the police.

"I thought my picture might be in the newspaper after I was dead, so I didn't want to look happy," she told me.

Janet had to help me walk out of there. A police escort took us to a nearby hotel to sleep for a few hours before taking us home. They knew the press would be waiting at our house.

* * *

WE ARRIVED AT MY HOME ABOUT NOON. The police had cordoned off our street, but the news media was gathered around our yard. Janet and I had no desire to speak with anyone. However, my father did. He was contacted by a separate reporter from the *Long Island Press* who inquired about how the ransom money was raised. My father said that managers at Bankers Trust were very helpful and that we had "mortgaged everything" to get the money. He also thanked the paper for not publishing the story until I was safe. "It was a wonderful thing to do," he said.

The next day he was interviewed again. "I have not seen Jack, but I talked with him on the phone last night for a minute," he said. "Yesterday was my birthday. I got him back on my birthday."

My father, Joe, and I were close. I was twenty-one years old when my mother died, and I lived with him until I married Janet. He never remarried and lived alone. After the incident, I couldn't bring myself to see him right away. It was too upsetting. I knew he was happy I was back. I felt so guilty about it. How could I not see him? But he didn't come see me, either. It was too emotional for him, too.

I finally pulled it together and visited him at 9 a.m. the next morning. We lived in the same town. His house was an eclectic ultramodern home built in the 1940s. Inside the front door was a large foyer with a long railing upstairs overlooking the ground floor. I let myself in. He wasn't down yet. When he heard me, he came to the upstairs banister fresh out of the shower and wearing a bathrobe. Our eyes locked. Without saying a word, he began bawling. I was his youngest child. In all my years I'd never seen him cry. He was a tough, street smart man from a much harder time. He was self-made, a fighter. But he had no control over what happened. His outpouring of emotion rattled me. I couldn't stay for long. It was too upsetting.

7

The Fortress

I had been delivered from captivity but was by no means free. The horrors of the kidnapping haunted me and will for the rest of my life. It never goes away. It's a trauma to cope with and overcome one day at a time. But out of that darkness came something special, something unforeseen. As much as the kidnappers had terrorized me and my family, the men and women who came to our defense brought solace. In their quest to protect us, they helped restore our strength. Some even became an intimate part of our lives—and still are.

The bond started within the first few days after my abduction. FBI Special Agent Joe Conley and Nassau County Det. Sgt. Frank Spinelli had moved into our home, along with FBI Special Agent Margot Dennedy. They brought suitcases with clothes. Or in law enforcement vernacular, they packed a lunch. These were serious people, dedicated to protecting the innocent from predators.

They'd put their lives at risk for us. Their specific task was to guard Janet and my children from danger morning, noon, and night. They were the first pillars of a fortress of protection that would last nearly a year.

Margot watched over Janet to great effect, Conley served us well, and Spinelli went out of his way in those early days to support Buddy. He had a job to do, but he also showed compassion for my wounded brother. Spinelli became Buddy's crutch. He guided and consoled Buddy throughout the ordeal. He was someone Buddy could talk to. At one point, Buddy broke down and cried on Spinelli's shoulder. He'd buckled under the pressure, but Spinelli kept him strong—that is, strong enough to get me back alive. Janet felt close to him too, and he was kind to me when I finally came home.

As time went on, it became deeply important for Janet and me to stay in touch with our fortress family. We would later become friends with Frank Spinelli and his wife.

As for the others, the bonds began forming in the months ahead.

Two separate but concurrent tracks emerged within the first moments of my debriefing at the FBI's midtown Manhattan headquarters. Both paths derived from the realization that the kidnappers had gotten away. On the one hand, a full-scale manhunt was underway. The FBI and Nassau County Police Department were committed to bringing the kidnappers to justice (more on that later). That required attention, resources, and manpower. On the other hand, there was an immediate need to secure my family's safety due to the very real possibility that the Keeper would make good on his threats to kill us if we went to the police. Within hours of my release, our pictures had been splashed across every newspaper and news program in the biggest media market in the country. The Keeper definitely knew Janet and I had crossed his red line.

With such emphasis on catching the kidnappers, I worried that the FBI and NCPD would leave us exposed. No one knew who the kidnappers were, and they'd already proven they could drive to my house, hold a gun to my head, and drive away unmolested. What's to stop that from happening again? What's to stop them from harming my wife or taking one of my children? After all, we were a proven source of money.

My concern was always my family. To his everlasting credit, Chief Curran kept his word to protect us. And they never charged me a dime.

After I came home, FBI agents and NCPD detectives guarded us around the clock. I had fallen into a deep depression. Today, we'd call it post-traumatic stress disorder. I was closed-off emotionally and unresponsive. I felt secure knowing officers were there, but I also knew I couldn't hide in my home forever. As difficult as it was, I decided to try to go back to work after about ten days. It was hard. I couldn't focus, but it was an important first step. I had to try to live again, even if it meant going through the motions. I don't know if I could've handled it without NCPD Detective Jim Garvey, who accompanied me to and from the office in those early days.

Janet was suffering, too. She looked to Chief Curran for answers. "How do we go on? How do I let my sons play outside or go to school?"

With a firm but caring bottom-line look, Curran raised his brow and told her, "If that's your attitude, then the only way to feel safe is to be locked up somewhere and never come out. Is that what you want?" She knew he was right, but moving on felt daunting. Janet had made a vow to herself to get me back. Now it was time to make another vow. She had to live again. She could not let herself succumb to fear. She couldn't let her sons grow up fearful either. The kidnappers terrorized us for a week, but there was no way Janet was going to let them shackle us with fear for the rest of our lives.

Soon, the FBI detail receded, but Nassau County allowed detectives to continue guarding us twenty-four hours a day, seven days a week. However, I knew that wouldn't go on forever, so I met with Chief Curran again to discuss a protection plan. He offered four to five permanent plainclothes policemen who would rotate shifts and provide constant security around the clock for the next several months. Then, we'd discuss whether I was comfortable eliminating the night shift in favor of a home alarm system. The plan involved paring down an unprecedented level of security, as needed, over the course of a year.

It was a strange but necessary way to live. If I went to work, an undercover policeman went with me. If Janet went grocery shopping with our children, a plainclothes officer would go with her. If Janet went out, a non-uniformed officer would escort her and another officer would stay at our house with the kids and me. They were all young men, younger than I was. One of the guys didn't want to be there, and it showed. "This is total nonsense. This is not what I signed up for. Let the detectives do it," he told the others. He wanted to be back in the field, not guarding some suburban family. But he was the exception.

The others made us feel safe while we recovered emotionally. They were fatherly and open to bonding with our kids. To this day, I feel guilty about not being more emotionally available during that time. I'm so glad the policemen were there.

Sometimes Janet would go bike riding while Marc was in school. She'd strap Michael into a baby seat, and an undercover officer would tag along. When winter came, one of the officers went outside and built a snowman with the boys. Another time, Janet bumped into a friend at a local supermarket. Dennis, her plainclothes escort, stood nearby with his gun visibly bulging from his pocket. Her friend assumed he was her "houseboy." She later confided in Janet that she assumed it was an interesting new trend in our family.

It wasn't safe to go out to restaurants or other places unless we had to, so Janet would cook at home, and the officers would eat with us. Lou, who often worked the evening shift, loved to cook. Sometimes he'd make dinner. They wore suits and civilian clothes and were under strict orders to protect us at all times and immediately report anything suspicious. Sometimes the arrangement felt normal. Then we'd be jolted back to reality by the beeps and static chatter on their two-way police radios or the sight of their guns.

These men integrated into our family and became our friends, even though they had a serious job to do. They weren't there for the fun of it. However, it developed into something special.

That's not to say there weren't trying times inside the fortress.

Marc was deeply affected by the occurrence of strange men rotating in and out of our house day and night. He was in second grade, and I wasn't around much, even when I was home. Janet was a nervous wreck and unable to give Marc unbroken attention. He was so young. Still, kids know when something isn't right, even if they can't understand it. Marc intuitively knew something was wrong and that he wasn't being told the truth.

"Where's my Dad?" he'd ask. "Why are you here and not my Dad?"

He didn't understand, and we couldn't tell him. It put the policemen in a tough spot, too. How were they supposed to respond? "Why are we here? Because your Daddy was kidnapped by anti-Semitic bad guys, and they might come back and hurt your family." No kid can process that, and no child deserves to have their innocence uprooted. But that was the situation. Marc struggled emotionally at school and regularly saw a therapist. The confusion would boil over into shouting and cries for help. "Why are they in my house? I want them to leave!" he'd yell. Once, Marc grabbed a knife and screamed at one of the officers, "Go away! Get out of here!" It was heartbreaking.

Janet and I saw a counselor as well. I was depressed, ornery, and short. The stress was at times unbearable for both of us. She ended up seeing another counselor on her own.

One of the men who was assigned to us after the first wave of federal agents and local detectives left was Joe Polimine. Joe and Marc got along well. He was a godsend. Joe was a young, working-class Italian from Brooklyn who, like me, had a young child at home. He spent nearly a year of his life with us and remains a close friend and part of our extended family today, more than forty-five years later.

Joe came from a good family and had a lot to live for. Yet, he carried a gun and was ready to throw himself in harm's way for us at the first sign of trouble. Over the course of that year, he became a close part of our family. He broke bread with us, stood guard while we slept, and even helped change Michael's diapers. It was a providential relationship that almost didn't happen.

Joe had grown up with aspirations of being a New York City cop. At eighteen, he took every recruitment test offered by the NYPD and the Port Authority police. Then he heard about a test for the Nassau County Police Department. A friend in the bookkeeping department at his downtown Manhattan job said her boyfriend was taking it.

"Nassau County? Where's that? Is that somewhere on Long Island?" he asked.

"Yes. And today is the last day," she said.

Joe told his boss he didn't feel well before skipping out to find out more about the test. He found the proper office and filed his paperwork with fingers crossed. But that was it. The actual test would come a year later, and by that time Joe was ready. He scored well on the psychological portion and passed his medical evaluation with flying colors, but the agility portion of the test was another story.

Each aspect was designed to weed people out, and there was only one hurdle left for him to cross, literally. The last agility metric required jumping over a rail without knocking it down. It made sense. Police officers run and jump over obstacles with heavy gear on every day in the New York metropolitan area. The test allowed three chances to make it over. The first time Joe tried, he knocked the rail off its posts. Same thing the second time. The third and final time, he bumped the rail again, but it jostled and bounced around on the crossbar brackets until it came to rest safely on the rail posts without hitting the ground.

"You passed," said the evaluator.

It was meant to be.

Joe promised himself that he'd take the first position offered no matter where it was. Then he received an NYPD offer and an appointment letter from the Nassau County Police Department at almost the same time. He had to choose. He lived in Brooklyn, so being a New York City cop made sense. It was convenient. It was his childhood dream. But before deciding, he took a trip across the Long Island Sound to Great Neck. He'd never been there before, he told me. "And you know what I saw? Trees. Lots and lots of trees. We didn't have trees in my neighborhood," he said.

Joe saw our side of life, and soon, I would get to know his.

Joe thought of his young family and chose Nassau County. He became a "footman." For nearly three years he patrolled the streets of the Sixth Precinct on foot. He'd walk into stores and introduce himself. He shook hands with people standing on corners. He got to know the people in our community. He also made arrests. It was neighborhood policing at its finest.

One day, his inspector called him into his office. "I have an assignment for you, Polimine. We have a security detail up in Kings Point."

"Kings Point, sir? Don't they have their own police department?"

The inspector explained the situation. "The Teich family...."

"Sure boss, whatever you need. Whatever they need."

"You'll wear civilian clothes. You'll be with the family at all times. Once you get there, they'll fill you in," he said.

It was mid-December when Joe arrived. I was in rough shape and wanted to know exactly who he was. Could I trust him? It would be hard for me to trust anyone for a long time, and there were other reasons to be unsure in those days. Prejudice was rampant, and Jews were no exception. Name calling, stereotypes, discrimination. Sometimes violence. The kidnappers were an extreme example, but casual anti-Semitism was everywhere. I wasn't going to allow it in my home. Not then, not ever. And definitely not after what I'd been through. Joe later shared that he was aware of such prejudices, and that his experience with us dispelled ugly stereotypes—not that he bought into them.

Similarly, I was determined not to become bitter about being targeted by men who happened to be black. You come to know people as individuals, you get close to them, and you see what they're really like. Religion and skin color have nothing to do with character.

The first thing that impressed Joe about Janet and me was how young we were. I imagine it was the same for the other policemen. After all the stories he'd heard about the kidnapping, he was floored that I wasn't an older man—which was interesting, considering Joe was just twenty-four at the time. I didn't talk to him right away. I was anxious, depressed, and angry. Social graces were the furthest thing from my mind. I could tell he felt bad for me but didn't know how to react. It was also uncomfortable to meet someone who knows you've been abused. There was nothing to talk about.

Over time we got more comfortable. I asked Joe about his job, his family, and where he came from. We got to know each other. He was carpooling from Brooklyn at the time with several other police officers who worked in Nassau County. One car, four cops. They often had to wait for Joe on their return evening trip home. His schedule was different from his footman days. If he was accompanying Janet to an appointment, or if some other security detail issue delayed him, he'd be late. It was causing him problems.

Joe began driving an old beat up car to our house. He was newly married and had a baby around Michael's age. He also had just bought a modest home. Joe was protecting me, so I decided to do something to protect him. I sold him my used Oldsmobile. He couldn't believe it.

It was a big brown Oldsmobile Delta 88. Joe sat in the front seat while guarding me, and I knew he liked the car. So I gave him a deal. It freed him up to travel safely and allowed him to use extra money for home heating oil that winter.

Later on, I took Joe and Frank Spinelli to the Aberdeen Proving Ground in Maryland. I'd been invited by the Army. For some reason they offered to let us drive Army tanks. It was a great time. I was able to laugh a bit. I remember having a moment to take it all in. I had escaped the evil of the tenement closet, and the murderous threats of the Keeper, and now, here I was with these men—driving Army tanks—who would take a bullet to protect my family if they had to. I felt grateful.

The first six months after my release was an unstable time that was balanced with protection and routine. Joe, Bob, Dennis, and Charlie—and John, an alternate officer on standby—would arrive at our house and park in the driveway. They drove their own cars, if they had one, rather than a squad car. The objective was to safeguard our family while we put our lives back together. The police didn't want us to stand out or to disrupt the neighborhood. The officers worked eight-hour, rotating tours. If Joe's weekly shift was 8:00 a.m. to 4:00 p.m., the following week he'd work 4:00 p.m. to midnight. The week after that, he'd work midnight to 8:00 a.m. and then go back to the daytime tour. The same applied to the other men.

Each time they came to the house, they'd check in on their radios. "Polimine is on. Dennis Delay is off. Copy?" Then they'd receive a briefing from the fellow they were relieving and find out what was—and wasn't—going on. They'd walk through each room, then around the house, and glance down the street for anything out of place, all while concealing .38-caliber handguns, also known colloquially as the Detective Special. Once they felt the area was secure, they came inside. Janet would have fresh coffee ready and took care of their meals.

The phones remained wiretapped. Only Janet was allowed to answer. If it was a friend, family member, or salesman calling, she could press a button, and the conversation would cease being recorded. If she went somewhere during the day, she'd drive, and the undercover policemen would sit in the passenger seat. In a store or in a parking lot, they'd trail her with a watchful eye and loaded gun. In crowded areas, they'd stick closer to her. It wasn't uncommon for Joe to pick up Michael as if he were his own child and tell Marc to stay close to him.

"If anything happens to this family, it's on me. I'm the guy," Joe said.

He took our safety personally. He tried to be as casual as he could while doing his utmost to protect us. Being a cop was his identity, but being a good cop meant everything. Joe was a good kid who was fearful of living with himself if he failed us. "Polimine, how could you let this happen? Why didn't you stop it?" He was determined to never face those questions.

At night, the policemen would flick on the television in the den to make it seem like there was activity inside the house. They'd draw the curtains to make sure the glowing screen could be seen from the street. They'd position themselves to see outside without being visible, and they'd watch for headlights. We lived on a cul de sac, so there was no reason to drive on our street unless you lived there or were visiting one of our neighbors, but occasionally cars drove up and down the road looking for an address they couldn't find. The officers would watch and wait until the cars would drive away without incident. They watched for walkers, but there were few. I was glad to know that for all the precautions there was no evidence of any threat. But I also knew it took less than two minutes to kidnap me.

The policemen were not part of the effort to capture the kidnappers, and they weren't privy to details of the ongoing investigation. But as time went on, Nassau County Detective Sergeant Dick McGuire would visit our house and speak with me about the case. Margot Dennedy would as well. My father, Joe, adored Margot.

My mother, Mary, died when I was young, and I had another brother. My mother was one of seven brothers and sisters born to Russian-American immigrants in 1904. She contracted rheumatic fever as a child and lived in a weakened state, often needing rest during the day. The ailment would eventually destroy one of her heart valves, which led to her death at age fifty-seven. Today, a routine operation would've saved her. Maybe Margot helped fill some of that family void for my father.

Margot was a compelling person, regardless. Like my father and Joe Polimine, she was pure Brooklyn. She was one of just five female FBI agents in the entire Bureau when she first arrived at our house during the week of my abduction. A few years later, Margot became the first female FBI supervisor in history. With such a male-dominated profession, she was once asked if she ever had any problems. Her answer? "None whatsoever. I'm from Brooklyn."

Getting close with Margot during that time of inner tumult added another unique life companion to our suburban bubble. She was a school teacher who went on to earn a graduate degree in history, only to be offered a secretarial position in corporate America. Margot was dating an attorney at the time who had previously served as an FBI agent himself before starting his own law practice. He encouraged Margot to give the FBI a shot. You can imagine how crazy that might have sounded, given that there were practically no female agents. But one of her former teaching friends also encouraged her after she became the only woman in the Queens District Attorney's Office. "You should do it," she told Margot.

Margot applied, was accepted, and ascended the ranks. She's never said anything negative about her thirty-year FBI experience, although during her early training in Quantico, Virginia, she constantly dealt with situations that were new for everyone. For instance, there were no female facilities, so occasionally a male trainee would stand outside the restroom door to block others from barging in. It was attention she did not seek. One time, an instructor screamed that Margot should toughen up and tried to get her to punch a cinder block wall. She was a pioneer, although she doesn't think of herself that way.

As these relationships were building inside our fortress of protection, outside an aggressive manhunt for the kidnappers was in full swing.

8

The Manhunt

While we did our best to reclaim normalcy inside the fortress, the FBI and Nassau County police conducted their manhunt for my kidnappers. In fact, without our knowledge, they had launched their massive effort just moments after I sat safely in the backseat of an unmarked Bureau car outside the Jade East Motel.

Fifty to sixty agents, detectives, and uniformed policemen had flooded the Jade East. Flashing red and blue lights were everywhere. More squad cars were on the way. A small army of law enforcement officials scoured the property and the surrounding area near Kennedy airport where the Keeper had dumped me. They took over the lobby, combed the guest registry, and demanded registration documents dating back several days before I was abducted. They knocked on the doors of all sixty-four units and peered inside, hoping to discern a connection on that cold November midnight. But nothing came of it.

Infighting had already begun. More than 450 federal, local, and city-wide law enforcement partners had tracked Janet and Buddy through Times Square and into Penn Station for the ransom payment. Some witnessed the pickup, and others watched the money-man stroll through one surveillance point after another until he disappeared. Despite their best efforts, the kidnapper and the ransom slipped away. How?

The official line was that the ransom-kidnapper was allowed to escape because it was too risky to follow him. This was true. But an unnamed FBI source leaked to the press that the man got away because of a critical technical oversight: no one tested the communication equipment prior to the surveillance operation. If they had, they would have discovered that the all-important radio transmitters didn't work underground. The station's steel beam framework and concrete walls rendered them all but useless.

Agents and officers continued to prowl my Long Island neighborhood, while others approached suspicious characters and groups throughout Times Square and Penn Station. The police detained several suspects in the early hours after my release. They had been spotted earlier that evening in a limousine that trailed behind Buddy's car on Broadway near 42nd Street. They were questioned, released, and wholly innocent.

From top brass to bottom-rung patrolmen, they worked their respective beats. They plotted strategies, interviewed informants, and searched for the tenement apartment where I was imprisoned.

The strongest lead, they believed, was that someone from inside Acme Steel Partition was involved—someone with knowledge that the company had access to large amounts of money and someone who knew my personal habits. I left the plant every day at the same time and went straight home. I never went to a bar after work or left early for a round of golf. I left around 6:30 p.m. every weekday and was home in time for dinner. But we had numerous employees, and not one of them stood out to me.

The FBI released a composite sketch of the man who picked up the ransom from the Penn Station locker. It depicted a bearded African-American male with glasses and a fedora-style hat. He reportedly stood about five feet, nine inches tall, weighed around 200 pounds, and was approximately forty years old.

The sketch wasn't very helpful. *What if the bag-man shaved?* I thought. What if he took the hat and glasses off? It could be almost any average-height, middle-aged man.

After some time, Janet and I decided to offer a reward. Our attorney, Martin Rosen, set up an organization that would shield our involvement and handle any incoming information. The police announced the $20,000 reward for information leading to the capture of the kidnappers and return of the ransom money.

Reward fliers outlined key aspects of the case: the kidnappers' noisy getaway car, the tenement apartment next to an elevated train, and the Keeper himself. "Anyone possessing information relative to the kidnapping is requested to contact the Nassau County Police Department or the Federal Bureau of Investigation. All information will be kept confidential," the fliers said.

Police also released a picture of the black ransom bag. The kidnappers had placed one of the bags in a trash can near Buddy's house, and an identical empty bag was in the coin-locker at Penn Station. The police announced they were looking to speak with anyone who might have sold two of the black bags to a single person.

A flurry of leads soon poured in, but all of them led to dead ends.

By mid-December, police had questioned dozens of suspects. But in each instance, the men were cleared and released.

The FBI also took me on a tour of car dealerships to match automotive similarities to identify the car used in my abduction. We looked at two-door cars, four-door cars, sports cars, and luxury sedans, both American and foreign. We looked at dozens of vehicles over the course of several days: Peugeot, Renault, Alfa Romero, Fiat, Triumph, Saab, a Camaro, an MG, a Jaguar Type 12.

We test drove all of them. I sat in the backseat trying to recall new information. "Does anything seem familiar? How about this one? This one over here?" I listened to the engines. Some were too quiet. Others were too loud. We examined headlights. But nothing seemed to ring a bell. We must have looked at more than forty cars.

Toward the end, we test-drove a Porsche 911. I sat in the back thinking it was a complete waste of time. *A Porsche? Really?* But the truth was that none of it was a waste. We had to do anything and everything to break the case. Somewhere in the back of my mind, there was a gnawing fear that the kidnappers might get away.

Sometime after my release, Buddy remembered two odd occurrences that had taken place before I was kidnapped. Both scenarios involved attempts to get him alone. The first happened in August three months prior to my abduction. A man named Larry Garrett had called Buddy and claimed he worked for the U.S. State Department. Garrett was supposedly representing "a government in exile" who needed steel doors and other steel building items. A meeting was arranged for 7:30 p.m.—the same time I was kidnapped—at the Westchester County Airport. Garrett said he would be traveling on a State Department airplane. But when Buddy arrived at the airport and searched for the appropriate terminal, he was informed that there were no State Department planes on the premises and that none were expected.

No one showed up to meet Buddy at the appointed rendezvous.

"I felt something was wrong," Buddy said. "It was an eerie sensation."

Police detectives thought a possible kidnapping plan may have been aborted because Buddy unwittingly brought his family, including our son, who had a sleepover at his house, and a large dog to the airport.

The following evening, Garrett called Buddy and apologized for not making it to the meeting. "We were all set to arrive in Westchester, but the plane had some last minute trouble flying out of Philadelphia," he said.

"I have an important package to deliver to you. We need you come back to the airport again and pick it up," Garrett added.

"What's in the package?" Buddy asked.

"Well, that's what we need you to come out there for. We can look at it together. It won't take long," Garrett said.

The back and forth persisted until Buddy reached his limit. "Enough! Tell me what's in the package, and stop the cloak and dagger stuff," he said.

Garrett became agitated at his response and hung up.

Buddy said it was strange but that he didn't know what to make of it. When he finally told the FBI during the manhunt, a background investigation revealed that there was no one named Larry Garrett who worked at the State Department, and that there was no evidence of any interest in contracting with Acme Steel Door and Partition Company.

The kidnappers tried to ensnare Buddy a second time about a month later. Someone called his home around midnight claiming to be a "Sergeant Muldoon" of the 94th Brooklyn police precinct where Acme Steel was located.

"Mister Teich, this is Sergeant Muldoon of the 94th Brooklyn police precinct. There's been a terrible accident at your company. One of your employees has been badly hurt, and we need you to come down here immediately and identify him."

We did have a night shift of workers at the plant at that time, but Buddy was instantly suspicious. My name, not his, was listed with the plant's security company.

"How did you get this number?" Buddy asked.

"Mister Teich, you're the only one we could reach tonight. This is serious. We need you to come down here and identify your employee. This is an emergency."

"Okay," Buddy replied. "Give me your number, and I'll call you right back. I'll find the right person to meet with you. They'll be there soon."

But the caller refused to give Buddy his number. He pressed for Buddy to give in but sounded less like a police officer with every try. The next day Buddy checked with the Brooklyn precinct. There was no Sgt. Muldoon to be found, and no one had been injured at the plant.

Detectives were convinced that Buddy's new information showed a deliberate conspiracy to kidnap a member of the Teich family by someone who had knowledge of Acme Steel Partition.

I became concerned about Buddy's safety. I had around-the-clock personal security. He didn't. Then again, he lived in Westchester County, not Nassau where Chief Curran vowed to protect my family. Since the kidnappers had gotten the ransom money, and Buddy wasn't the ultimate victim, the bet was that they wouldn't come back and hurt him. But there were no guarantees.

As the investigation continued, several weeks after my release I received a call at home from the investigators.

"Jack, would you mind coming into the FBI office in Manhattan? We'll pick you up. Inspector Guido would like to see you."

Inspector Daniel Guido was one of the smartest, most decent men I met during that period. Guido was razor sharp. He had a brilliant law enforcement mind. He was always thinking, always a few steps ahead. He saw the big picture and methodically filled in the blanks. He would be promoted to commissioner during the course of the investigation, and in turn, he'd promote Det. Dick McGuire. The two of them sank their teeth into my case and never let go.

An agent from my home security detail drove me to FBI headquarters. Guido was waiting patiently.

"Hello, Jack. Let's spend some time together. Just you and me. Would that be okay?"

"Fine," I said.

Guido wanted to know everything. Things I knew, things I wasn't sure about, and things I didn't know. I had already been interviewed for dozens of hours, but Guido wanted to go deeper. Every detail was important to him. That was his attitude.

"What was the temperature in the closet, Jack?"

"Was there any squeaking in the floorboards of the apartment?"

"Were they wooden floors? What type of wood? Were they soft? Hard?"

"What other sounds did you hear? What about sounds from the street?"

"How about smells? Inside smells? Outside smells? Smells when you walked into the building? Out of the building?"

At one point we broke for lunch. There was an excellent kosher style deli on the same street.

"What do you want, Jack? I've got this," Guido said, handing me a menu.

"A corned beef sandwich," I said, without looking. I loved corned beef sandwiches. Always have. We waited until someone finally brought the food. I took one bite, but couldn't swallow. I couldn't eat. I was too upset.

Guido finished his food and started asking detailed questions again. I did my best to answer. I don't know if any of it helped. I just know I left completely drained.

A short time later I received another call. "Inspector Guido would like to see you again."

"Jack, in cases like this, we want to eliminate any possibility that we're wrong or that we don't know everything that's going on," said Guido. "So we're asking you and Buddy to take a polygraph test."

I knew what a polygraph was. I had never taken one, but I knew it was a lie-detector test. I wasn't lying, so I figured what's the big deal? "Sure, I'll take it," I said. The test was a frozen moment where I couldn't believe what my life had come to.

The polygraph was taxing.

"Jack, did you take the money? Do you know the kidnappers? Did you fake your own disappearance?"

The test was to determine whether Buddy and I cooked up my own kidnapping and then lied to the police about it. The polygraph examiner probed my personal life, the company's finances, and whether Buddy and I were extorting money from my father.

I came out clean as a whistle, of course, as did my brother Buddy.

As weeks turned to months, the police were still contacting me to revisit old leads. FBI agents and police detectives believed the kidnapping lair was critical to the investigation, and they narrowed it down to somewhere in the Fordham and Tremont sections of the West Bronx. I already told them about the address on a paper coffee cup. That information came from a hypnosis session.

Fordham and Tremont were consistent with the tollgate and steep hill along the path from my driveway to the apartment, and the elevated train line I heard while chained to the bed. The tollgate and corresponding drive-time mostly ruled out Brooklyn and Queens. The police felt like the kidnappers wouldn't have taken a roundabout trip either to the Southern State Parkway or through the Rockaways just to introduce a tollgate red herring. It's much more likely, they surmised, that they took the Throgs Neck Bridge from Long Island to the Cross Bronx Expressway to the Bronx. Plus, the eight-by-eight-foot room with two-by-five-foot closet and single window is standard for many of the abandoned tenements in the West Bronx.

I drove with agents and detectives many evenings listening to the sounds...trying to recognize anything familiar to the place where I had been held. I even rode nearly all night with Assistant FBI Director John Malone trying to find the location in the Bronx. They looked and looked, but it was all for naught. They didn't find the apartment.

Months later, I received a call at my office. The voice immediately reminded me of the Keeper. It was uncanny. It wasn't the Keeper, but the voice reminded me of him. My blood ran cold. The police had asked since the beginning if I could provide more information about the main kidnapper's voice. "What was the voice you heard? Can you describe it?" It was always difficult for me to explain. Now, I could point to a similar voice.

I rushed to call the police and told them that the man's tone and verbal cadence reminded me of the Keeper. "It wasn't a Southern accent, New York accent, or foreign accent. It was a clear speaking voice. He thought before he spoke, and he spoke with a distinct intelligence. He was articulate. He didn't use slang," I explained.

I was so excited, but I was grasping at straws. Long periods were passing by without any updates. It was confounding.

On the one-year anniversary of the kidnapping, reporters began contacting me for comment. "What's new, Jack? Are you still confident the police will find your kidnappers? What can you say about the case?" they asked.

What could I say about the case? I didn't know anything new. I didn't know if the police did, either. And I wouldn't have told them anyway. I was reluctant to speak. It was still too dangerous as far as I was concerned. The Keeper's threats were clear, and he was still out there, somewhere. Plus, I wasn't about to compromise the investigation, and I was trying to move on with my life.

One thing I did know, however, was that hundreds of law enforcement officials were initially assigned to hunting down the kidnappers. Now, a year later, hundreds had dwindled into a handful. The case was a mystery, even though Chief Curran was telling the press that Nassau County police were still fielding plenty of leads.

A year and a half later, there'd been no visible progress at all. The FBI had reduced its commitment to just five agents. Only Nassau County detectives were working on the case full-time.

"To be truthful, we never really got off the ground, Jack," said Chief Curran. "We haven't located the place of confinement. That would have been a big help."

9

The Break

For nearly two years, the authorities reported no progress on the investigation. They answered questions, fewer and fewer over time, but offered little in the way of new information. There were no outward signs of any breakthroughs or imminent arrests. The initial intensity and outside interest had mostly died off, but Commissioner Danny Guido and Detective Dick McGuire knew a lot more than they told the press—and me.

It took a while, but they quietly got their break.

The first area of interest had always been Acme Steel Partition. Who would've known about the employee profit sharing fund? Someone on the inside. Only a few of us knew the details of the account, such as how much was in it, where it was held, and how accessible it was. Then again, everyone at the company knew the fund existed. They wouldn't have known big picture details, but they were either invested in the fund or had the opportunity to do so.

We furnished the FBI and the police with a list of 600 past and present workers. They quickly began whittling off non-starters and conducted exploratory interviews with anyone who might have the thinnest of connections to the case. One former employee caught their early attention: Charles Berkley.

Berkley worked at Acme Steel Partition for fifteen years as a draftsman before leaving the company to start his own business. When he left, he withdrew $12,000 in profit sharing to fund his new venture. That was almost two years before my abduction. They asked me about him, and I said it didn't make sense. "There's no way Charles Berkley was involved."

He was a family man who was married with four children. He had also served in the Korean War as a paratrooper and was a longtime stable employee. He didn't leave on bad terms, either. Berkley wasn't fired. He left to go out on his own. More power to him, I thought. We wished him luck and no hard feelings. People come, people go.

But apparently, things didn't go well. Berkley was a skilled drafts-man, not businessman. And curiously, the business he chose had nothing to do with drafting or anything similar. He went into real estate and closed shop in just three months. From there, he joined a competitor of Acme Steel Partition. After a period of months, he left unsatisfied and joined another competitor, Superior Fire Door Co. in Westchester County. I knew the owner. Berkley started at Superior Fire Door in late-1973 and was attempting to get re-hired at Acme Steel Partition when I was kidnapped.

I never thought twice about it. He'd tried his hand in business, and it didn't work out. No big deal.

Nassau County police detectives, however, did think he was a big deal—not that they told me at the time. Berkley was questioned on December 12, 1974, almost three weeks after I was released from the tenement apartment. The pre-interview background investigation was impressive. His out-of-left-field real estate venture was odd, but further scrutiny showed inconsistencies and an overall lack of clarity regarding his real estate business, its location, and the partners involved.

Detectives thought it was of note that Berkley's parents were of West Indian extraction, and that he was a shop steward who was active in employee disputes and union matters. Anonymous coworkers at Superior Fire Door also told police that he argued about controversial social issues.

But an unsettling discovery showed Berkley had a side I'd never seen. I was part owner and vice president of Acme Steel, so I didn't know him well, but he'd always seemed nice enough. Turns out, Berkley had surreptitiously distributed "black nationalist" literature at Acme. Several workers gave investigators written materials Berkley had handed out years earlier. He authored one item called, "Black Thoughts on Green Power." It's a poorly reasoned anti-Semitic treatise that begins strangely and segues into the plight of German Jews.

> *Green Power can get you food, clothes, big or little cars, roller skates, stocks and bonds, baseball bats, dogs and cats, married, whiskey, fur coats, a Bible, marijuana, bailed out of jail, a formal education, black or white prostitutes, furniture, chocolate covered ants, steaks in the backyard, tickets to rock concerts and basketball games, a lawyer, your hair straightened, elected to public office and a head stone. Green Power can get you in the Masons, the American Legion, the Playboy Club, the Elks, the Knights of Columbus, and the Pinky Dinks and N.A.A.C.P.*

It continues:

> *Believing the wealth and position [the Jews] had attained was sufficient to survive eternally, and blinded by the gold that glittered, most Jews refused to listen and take heed of at first the racist rhetoric and then the outright acts of terror committed against them by the Germans. There is no need to repeat the history of how the Jew in Germany was exterminated.*

Today, gold is as much a part of the Jews life as it ever was, however, since the Jews tragic days in Germany, he has not been blinded by gold.

The many Black advocates of Green Power, who believe the Black Man's only way of 'making it' (whatever making it is suppose to mean), reminds one of the blinded Jews. I suppose, if one is willing to stay in ones place and forget about the freedoms denied Black people in this and other lands, Green Power for them is all that matters. A prostitute sells her flesh, some people sell their souls.

Berkley also selectively gave out fliers advertising a Co-Op City, Bronx, play he starred in in 1971. The play, called "Elegy to X," was part of a ceremony invoking "the spirit of Malcolm X." It opens with Amiri Baraha's "A Poem for Black Hearts".

But what did any of this prove? That Berkley was a reliable employee with a nasty side? That's not a crime, nor was it an evidentiary link to my kidnapping. At most, Berkley had cursory knowledge of the employee fund and shared a strain of the kidnappers' demented ideology.

Nothing came of the interview, although Berkley was floated as an early unnamed suspect to the media. He mostly faded from interest as the months dragged on.

* * *

McGuire took it upon himself to follow up another early outlier of a detail—the odd calls Buddy received. The man who had called pretending to be a "Larry Garrett of the U.S. State Department" had wanted Buddy to meet him at the West Air terminal of the Westchester County Airport. So, with an FBI agent in tow, McGuire drove to the Westchester County Airport north of the Bronx to conduct an interview. He'd perused airport and West Air employee records looking for anyone with a criminal background and settled on a meet-and-greet subject. It was readily apparent the airport worker had nothing to do with my case. He was helpful and introduced McGuire to a fellow coworker, but he didn't know anything either.

McGuire thanked them, and it was back to the drawing board. When escorting the two lawmen back to the main terminal, the FBI agent pointed and said, "What the hell kind of plane is that?"

"It's a push-pull," one of the employees said. "Beechcraft. Looks kinda funny doesn't it? It's got an engine in the front and an engine in the back. Some guys use them to get two licenses. It has two engines, but it's really like flying a single-engine plane."

It was a throw-away factoid, small talk on the way out. Then out of nowhere, the air worker said, "You know, the guy that owns it is a black guy whose kid was kidnapped."

McGuire stopped dead in his tracks. "Excuse me?"

"The guy that owns that push-pull. His kid was kidnapped a while ago. That's what I heard."

McGuire hadn't mentioned my kidnapping. He'd only probed about Larry Garrett and anything else that might've fit the bill for an ambush against Buddy. When they got inside, McGuire asked to review the plane records. It was registered to a Mr. Rudy Williams of Westchester County.

* * *

Detective Sergeant McGuire and FBI Special Agent Richard Staedtler traveled to Greenburgh, New York, in western Westchester County to surprise interview Rudy Williams. They knocked on his door. Williams answered.

"Mister Williams, my name is Detective Sergeant Richard McGuire. This is FBI Special Agent Richard Staedtler. Can we come in?"

Williams stood halfway behind the door, looked them up and down suspiciously, and said, "No."

"How do I know you're who you say you are?" he added.

An interesting response, McGuire thought. Williams was clearly irritated, but he wasn't rejecting an interview.

McGuire, of course, had done his homework. Williams' house was valued at approximately $100,000, which was more than mine. It sat on a hilltop in a posh neighborhood and was listed under the name Gwendolyn Dent. The home interior appeared to be expensively furnished from McGuire's initial impression at the door.

Williams spoke after a prickly pregnant pause. "I'm calling the cops to check you out." He closed the door abruptly and locked it.

While McGuire and Staedtler waited outside, an African-American female pulled into the driveway. She got out, walked to the house, and keyed the front door. Stares were exchanged but no words. McGuire spied a mirror reflection when the door swung open, a third person—an African-American male standing roughly five feet, nine inches, wearing a wide-brimmed hat and multi-colored clothes. The door slammed shut without the reflection revealing a face.

Williams opened the door several minutes later. "Come in," he said with a flippant wave. He led his uninvited guests to a large sitting area where the three men sat for an awkward interview.

"Mister Williams, will you please state your place of employment?"

"I don't have to answer that. Next question," he responded.

"Is this your permanent residence?"

"What's that got to do with anything. You accusing me of something? Or you want to talk about someone else?" Williams retorted.

McGuire paused and gave a brief summary of my kidnapping. He said he was interviewing Williams because of certain similarities.

"Similarities? Like what?" Williams asked.

"Similarities, Mister Williams, as in you were a victim of an attempted ransom extortion plot in May 1974, were you not?" McGuire proposed.

"Yes."

"Can you talk to us about that? What was the nature of the kidnapping? Who were the individuals who may have been involved?" asked McGuire.

"I don't know," Williams said tersely.

"Look, I'm sorry this other guy got kidnapped. I hope he's ok. But I don't know anything about it, and that's all I have to say," he added.

McGuire and Staedtler looked at each other. The interview was over.

"One last thing, Mister Williams. Do you recognize any of these individuals?"

McGuire handed Williams a half-dozen portrait photographs and a copy of the composite sketch of the Penn Station ransom bagman. One of the men in the portrait pile was Charles Berkley.

"Nope. I don't know any of these people. Don't know any of them at all," he said, handing back the pictures.

McGuire studied Williams. He took in the moment knowing how he'd arranged the photos. His gut told him Williams was lying.

"When you show a guy with a past six pictures, he usually goes one of two ways: 'No, no...maybe this guy...no, no...no.' Or he'll quickly say, 'No, no, no. Got nothing for ya,' when you put someone in there they definitely know," McGuire later explained.

He let Williams slide and smoothly ended the interview. Then, he stood up and dropped the polite persona.

"Here's the deal, pal. I'm gonna check on you. You've got a long rap sheet. Lots of gambling convictions," McGuire started.

"You're gonna need a favor someday, and when you do, call me. Understand? When you get in trouble again, you call me. We'll talk."

Williams had been played, and he knew it.

* * *

As TIME DRAGGED ON, the initial promise of the Charles Berkley and Rudy Williams leads fizzled into backburner persons of interest. Det. Sgt. McGuire and Commissioner Guido were frustrated. Worse, the FBI was getting ready to pull the plug on the investigation. They'd committed an unusual amount of manpower and financial resources without results.

It was a harsh reality check: the investigation could not go on forever—not actively. Some crimes go unsolved, and this just may be one of those cases. The thought burned McGuire. An FBI supervisor, Agent Leo McGillicuddy, called him early one morning with bad news. "Dick, they're getting nervous upstairs. We're about to start unwinding this thing, as there is no evidence of interstate involvement."

McGuire called Commissioner Guido. "Listen boss, this isn't looking good. They're about to pull it."

Guido was just as determined as his top Jacknap detective. They were kindred spirits in that they're the type of people who never give up. Never. Some men fight the good fight and when it's time to hang it up, they walk away. And some men never quit. That's McGuire and Guido. I'm forever grateful to them.

Guido arranged a sit-down to discuss the future of the case. He was adamant that they'd catch the kidnappers if they just kept going. He believed it. Guido had the vision for success, and he urged decision makers not to wave the white flag at the investigation's lowest point. Guido was a real leader. His efforts led to a compromise. An agreement was made to cut back on my home security detail and adopt a joint FBI-NCPD skeleton crew of investigators. The several FBI counterparts would work on a part-time basis, and McGuire and his partner, Det. Jim Moran, would be allowed to continue full time.

Soon after, the break came.

It was Rudy Williams. He wanted to meet with Det. Sgt. McGuire again.

"Dick, I got this guy, says he knows you." It was an old detective friend calling from Greenburgh, New York. McGuire had helped him solve a homicide years earlier involving a multi-county burglary ring. The detective owed McGuire a favor and called to deliver.

"Says he knows something about your case. I don't know if he's just talkin' to talk or—"

"Is it Rudy Williams?" McGuire asked.

"Yeah. How'd you know?"

McGuire had poured his life into finding my kidnappers for a year and half. It was his personal mission. His wife would find him awake in the middle of the night reviewing notes and journaling about possible leads. The idea that he'd randomly guess Rudy Williams was a bit irksome.

"Because I know," he said.

Rudy Williams was one of many hooks McGuire had baited in the hopes of getting a bite. He'd been patiently waiting for these types of calls.

"Tell him to call me," McGuire said.

They arranged an evening meeting at a Westchester County hotel bar. McGuire arrived on time and entered the darkened lounge. Teddy Pendergrass was playing in the background. He spotted Williams sitting with a young woman. He'd been drinking.

"Let's have a drink," Williams said.

McGuire ordered a drink to put Williams at ease. "What's up, Rudy? How's things?"

"Things are things. What do you got for me?" he said.

Williams had gotten busted for a gun. He was facing prison time and wanted a deal. He knew McGuire would be up-to-speed.

"That depends," said McGuire. "Here's how it works. You tell me everything, and I'll see what I can do. If you hold back or lie to me, it's over. You're gone. This is your one shot. What do you have for me, Rudy?"

Williams paused and said, "Those pictures you showed me. Remember? I know one of those guys. His name's Charles Berkley."

McGuire held his gaze and stared straight into Williams's eyes. His countenance revealed nothing. He remembered slipping Berkley's picture in the photos. But Rudy Williams recognizing Charles Berkley didn't prove anything. McGuire already knew about Berkley, and there'd been no movement on that front.

"What else?" said McGuire. "What else, Rudy?"

Williams sipped his drink and took a deep breath. "The other guy. I can damn near give 'em to you."

"Which other guy?" said McGuire.

"The drawing."

McGuire's heart skipped a beat. He shivered from a surge of adrenaline. It was all he could do to not give away his excitement.

"Yeah. I'm listening," he said.

Williams paused. He was holding out for a return promise to keep him out of jail. But McGuire wasn't having it, and he couldn't make that promise anyway.

"Don't dare me, Rudy. I'm telling you right now, don't play games with me. You're not gonna like it. I'm the only thing standing between you and prison, and I'm walking out of here in ten seconds," he said.

Williams threw back his drink and postured. Then he said, "The drawing. That's my brother, Richard Williams. He went to high school with Charles Berkley. They're friends."

If true, McGuire knew this could be it. This could be the game. It was the best lead he'd come by in countless hours of pounding the pavement and scouring files around the clock.

"Okay, Rudy. I believe you. Sit tight," McGuire said. "Don't leave town. I'll see what I can do."

* * *

McGuire dug in with renewed vigor. Richard Williams...Richard Williams...His mind churned over the new lead. Was it bullshit or the real thing? He enlisted help in checking Richard Williams's background. The results were stunning.

Richard Warren Williams, forty-three, was born in Brooklyn, New York. He went to Needles Trade High School in the Fort Greene area. Today, it's called Brooklyn Tech. Records showed that Charles Berkley also attended Needles, which added credibility to Rudy Williams's tip.

Like Berkley, Richard Williams served in the Korean War after high school. But he left Brooklyn in 1959, long before my kidnapping. He wanted a better life, apparently, and decided to cast his lot in sunny California. He opened a real estate agency in Los Angeles, where he specialized in selling homes to black and Hispanic clientele in the mostly all-white San Fernando Valley. By all accounts, he'd became a successful real estate entrepreneur.

Richard Williams seemed the epitome of the American Dream—not the kind of person who would mastermind an anti-Semitic-fueled kidnapping. His firm became one of the fastest growing real estate businesses in Southern California. He hired African Americans and Hispanics at a time when those groups were often locked out of good jobs. He became wealthy. Records showed he bought a plane, obtained a pilot's license, and lived in a $100,000 home. He was a legitimate leader in the Los Angeles African-American community.

But there were plenty of cracks beneath the surface. At the height of his success, Richard Williams veered into black militancy. Despite not having a college degree, he was invited to teach at California State University, Northridge, about twenty-five miles from downtown L.A. It was 1969, and afro-militancy was a fringe ideology that gained traction in certain corners of college campuses, the California university system being ground zero. Williams became radicalized during his teaching stint and began hanging pictures of political radicals in his office, like Angela Davis and Malcolm X. Customers and employees were put off by the overt extremism, and his blossoming real estate empire abruptly collapsed.

Williams then left the country and relocated to Guyana, on the northeast coast of South America. The small Caribbean-bordering nation had gained its independence in 1966. Since the early nineteenth century, the former British colony functioned as a smattering of large sugarcane plantations that were serviced with African slave labor. Now it was free, and presumably Williams saw an entrepreneurial opportunity. He attempted to launch an airplane shuttle service from Guyana to the United States, but the plan never took off. Ironically, Williams became frustrated with the country's socialistic restrictions on business and returned to Los Angeles dead-broke in the spring of 1974.

As McGuire and Guido were putting these pieces of the Jack-nap puzzle together from information flowing in from both coasts, another major break surfaced.

"Danny," McGuire said to Commissioner Guido, his boss, "send me to California."

10

The Money Trailer

Commissioner Guido wanted to send McGuire to California but couldn't—not at first. Department finances had been scaled back, and Guido's hands were tied. It killed McGuire, but the Los Angeles FBI first approached Richard Williams for an interview. He'd have given anything to be there to see the look in his eyes. "Hi, Richard. The name Jack Teich mean anything to you?"

The pieces fit. Of course, Williams denied everything. He claimed total ignorance. And the FBI had no hard evidence to show otherwise. Not yet.

Back in New York, McGuire and Guido were making the best of a tough situation. Within two weeks of contact with Williams, they arrived at another breakthrough. They needed to link Richard Williams and Charles Berkley beyond the word of Williams's convict brother. A review of phone records appeared to do the trick—but not Berkley's home phone records. They had already tried that. Instead,

McGuire asked Berkley's former employer for a list of unusual long distance phone numbers from June 1973 through December 1974—a period well-before and just after my kidnapping.

A representative from Superior Fireproof Door and Sash Company provided the information, which included thirteen unique numbers that couldn't be explained. Why would someone from the Scarsdale, New York, business call Los Angeles? More specifically, Hawthorne, California, an area near LAX? Was there a plausible explanation? The company's office manager was at a loss.

"I don't recognize any of this," he said. "It doesn't make sense to me."

McGuire bee-lined to Guido. Williams lived in Hawthorne.

"Danny, we've got to get going. We need to get the D.A.'s office involved, now. We can't wait any longer."

Together, they approached the district attorney's chief assistant, Henry Devine. They'd all slogged through the trenches on previous cases, and Devine liked them. Guido made the policy argument. McGuire appealed to his manhood.

"Listen Henry, here's the deal," said McGuire. "You've known me a long time, and I don't bullshit anybody. We need a really good D.A., somebody we can work with, who understands what we're doing. There's no time to screw around."

Devine thought about it. He'd have to answer to the D.A. Justice was always the priority, but there were other considerations. The D.A. answers to voters, and voters are influenced by the press. Was this a winnable case? How would it play out in the papers?

"Alright, Dick. I've got just the guy for you. Let me introduce you to Ed McCarty."

Ed McCarty was razor sharp, but he was young. He was in his early thirties and had a reputation for working strictly by the book. *"If this case goes forward,"* McGuire thought, *"can I live with this guy? Could he prosecute the biggest case in Nassau County history?"*

McGuire had no choice.

One thing that inspired confidence was that McCarty was an overachiever. When other prosecutors were taking it easy, McCarty was out looking for an edge. He asked the county medical examiner to mentor him when he wasn't litigating, for instance. He wanted an advantage over his opponents in future cases. By his mid-thirties, McCarty had seen so many autopsies that he could've performed one.

A few years after I first met McCarty, he was asked by the county political establishment to run for a judgeship. The same week, he received an offer from a high-profile medical malpractice law firm. He chose the judgeship. When his medical examiner mentor found out, he called McCarty and said, "Ed, you know that decision cost you ten million dollars?"

"Yeah," he replied. "But you take your own directions in life."

That's Ed McCarty.

* * *

By June 1976, Guido had wrangled enough funding to send McGuire to California. The FBI was barely committed at that point, so Guido managed to send Detective Jim Moran along to assist McGuire. They landed in Los Angeles on Father's Day. They decided to eat at the airport before launching into the investigation. The grizzled New York detectives struggled to find an acceptable food stop. They settled on a restaurant that looked like a spaceship.

"Let's just say the menu was short on steak and potatoes," McGuire later recalled. "It was all salads. I ordered a spinach salad. Shit, I'd never done that before. I told them to find bacon for it."

McGuire and Moran left the airport, holstered their firearms, and pocketed law enforcement permit papers. They'd come in handy if stopped by LAPD. They spent the rest of the day pursuing leads from Berkley's employment phone records and Richard Williams's former real estate business. They met the FBI's Los Angeles point man, Special Agent Doug Ball.

The feds had a general air of superiority, but it was rarely a problem. Most of them respected local law enforcement, but McGuire felt like the L.A. Bureau blew him off. They didn't think a detective from

Long Island was going to drop in for a few weeks and solve a dormant kidnapping case. Doug Ball was different.

"Okay, Dicky. Let's do it, man. We're gonna find these guys," he said.

Ball had a plan. He knew exactly what to do. He'd handle surveillance while the New York detectives pounded pavement and developed human intel.

"Okay, Doug," said McGuire. "You're my main man. But listen, we already reached out to the D.A. He turned us down. So let's keep our eyes open, because things are going to start rolling. Trust me."

Outside of Ball, McGuire, and Moran, they were on their own. The L.A. County District Attorney's Office wouldn't even meet with them, and McCarty was three thousand miles away in another jurisdiction. But they knew they had the right suspects in Richard Williams and Charles Berkley.

Their first interview was with Leroy Don Darrett, a former employee at Ric Williams Realty. Darrett, an African-American, said business was good until Williams left to teach Black History at Cal State Northridge. "He changed," said Darrett.

"Ric said he was proud of being his own boss and that he didn't have to work for 'whitey,'" said Darrett. "He spoke like that all the time."

He told McGuire that Williams began putting African figurines around the office, as well as posters of political extremists. "Ric idolized Chickenman. He was some kind of rebel who taught Caribbean islanders how to grow crops," said Darrett.

"I told him, 'Ric, this is hurting the business.' He said, 'It's my office, and I'll do as I please. You don't tell me!'" He also said Williams began carrying a loaded .32 caliber pistol around that time.

McGuire and Moran moved to another former employee named Gloria Larkin. She said Williams disappeared in 1971 and that he owed her money. But in September 1974, he resurfaced as abruptly as he'd left. Larkin said she pursued the debt and was surprised when Williams paid her. She remembered receiving $400 with a four-page letter attached signed, "Kufanya."

Then, in January 1975, Larkin said she got a phone call from Williams asking her to dinner. "He looked nervous. He said the CIA, FBI, and police were after him. I asked him what for, and he wouldn't talk about it," she explained. Without solicitation, Larkin offered that Williams—whom she knew to have financial problems—paid for the dinner with a one-hundred-dollar bill.

Larkin said she couldn't identify Williams from the New York police artist sketch, but said he was extremely smart, well-organized, and very militant. "Ric would say the 'establishment' was the reason for black people's problems," she said.

As one lead led to another, McGuire and Moran met with a former Ric Williams Realty employee who was so burned by his employment experience that he agreed to sign a written statement. The New York detectives played tape recordings of the November 1974 ransom calls to my wife, Janet. The man's jaw dropped. "I immediately recognized the voice of the man demanding the money as my former employer, Ric Williams. I have no doubt as to the identity of the voice," he attested.

A week later, McGuire and Moran located Williams's brother-in-law, Earl Fields. He claimed no knowledge of anyone named Charles Berkley, but added Williams liked to go by his African name, Kufanya. Fields also said that Williams, who was married, had a girlfriend named Marie Washington.

McGuire requested a records check on Washington, which yielded another breakthrough. Washington had an Exxon credit card. From August 2 to August 9, 1974, a clear path of gas station purchases was made in an apparent cross country road trip. The trail of gas purchases began in Lennox, California, just east of LAX, and proceeded in a northeasterly direction. First Barstow, then Needles, California, followed by Seligman and Flagstaff, Arizona; then Cuervo, New Mexico; Amarillo, Texas; Tulsa, Oklahoma; Joplin, Missouri; Terre Haute, Indiana; Somerset, Pennsylvania; and Plainfield Station, New Jersey.

Last stop, Larchmont, New York—the place where my brother, Buddy, lives and also the place where the kidnappers left the ransom bag in the trash can at the Exxon station.

An extended timeline of gas purchases shows a distinct split. From October 28 through the end of my kidnapping on November 22, 1974, Marie Washington was making Exxon credit card purchases back in Los Angeles. The gas purchases were tied to the same vehicle that had previously journeyed cross-country, California license plate 865 ETO. But Marie's husband, someone who went by the name, "James Washington," was making Exxon credit card purchases during the same time period in Springfield Gardens, New York—a Queens neighborhood next to JFK airport.

Apparently, there were two Exxon cards and two vehicles. The vehicle "James Washington" used had a New York license plate, 482 QUA. According to the New York State Department of Motor Vehicles, that car was a two-door 1965 Ford Mustang. It also happened to be registered to a young woman named Celestyne Williams, the daughter of Richard Warren Williams.

McGuire had found the kidnapping car.

What's more, three Exxon gas purchases on November 24, 1974, indicated another road trip, this time in a third car heading due south. The first credit card entry was in New York, and the third was at a gas station in Battleboro, North Carolina, at I-95. Connecting the dots gave the impression of an escape route.

With the information in hand, on July 8, 1976, an FBI agent under the direction of Doug Ball approached the owner of Williams's Hawthorne, California, apartment complex. The owner confirmed that "James Washington" rented an apartment from him and said Washington always paid in cash. He added that Washington lived with his wife, Marie, and that they left during the summer of 1974, came back the next month, and left again in October 1974.

At the end of the interview, the agent brandished a photograph of Richard Williams. "Yep, that's him," the apartment complex owner said. "That's James Washington." It was an alias. "James Washington" was Richard Williams.

McGuire and Moran had since returned to New York, but not before driving more than two thousand miles and conducting dozens of interviews while in Los Angeles. By late July, McGuire had located Celestyne Williams, who went by her married name, Celestyne Glenn. He dropped by her Jamaica, Queens, apartment for a surprise visit.

"Missus Glenn, my name is Detective Sergeant Richard McGuire. I'd like to talk with you about a 1965 Ford Mustang and your father, Richard."

Williams-Glenn reacted emotionally and refused to let McGuire inside. He'd touched a nerve. McGuire diffused the situation and got her to agree to listen to a tape recording of one of the ransom calls. He waited outside the apartment door. She returned two minutes later and said that the recording, "sounds like an Israeli newscast."

When asked about the 1965 Ford Mustang, Williams-Glenn said, "I won't answer that, and I don't know. I don't have to answer. All I have to do is die and pay taxes, right?"

McGuire reminded her that she had told the FBI in February 1976 that she hadn't seen her father in five years.

"It's not good to lie to the FBI, Missus Glenn," said McGuire.

"Well, I guess that's what I said then," she answered and slammed the door.

* * *

AGENT DOUG BALL HAD BEEN TRAILING Williams for months. He was still living by LAX and was going about his business without so much as jaywalking—until August 18.

"Dicky! Dicky, we got one. We got one!"

"Slow down, Doug. What do mean 'we got one?'" asked McGuire. He'd stepped out from a briefing at NCPD headquarters in Mineola, Long Island, to take the call. It was Doug Ball.

"We got a bill, Dicky. A one-hundred-dollar bill with a matching serial number. It's ransom money," said Ball.

McGuire instantly felt the gravity of the discovery.

"Williams paid his rent with it," said Ball.

"That's great, Doug. That's really great. I'll tell Danny [Guido]. Keep on 'em. We're close."

It was cause for celebration. Connecting Williams to a ransom bill was hard evidence, but McCarty wasn't jumping for joy. He'd have to prosecute the case. He needed more.

Ball placed Williams under around-the-clock surveillance hoping he'd drop more ransom bills—which he did.

On September 3, Williams spent another one-hundred-dollar bill with a matching serial number at a Los Angeles tire store. The store manager said the bill was passed by a man named C.R. Lee. Williams was known to use multiple aliases, including Charles R. Lee. It was another piece of the puzzle.

Two days later, Williams spent yet another matching one-hundred-dollar bill at a Santa Monica grocery store. He was going out of his way to use the bills at unrelated locations. A cashier at the supermarket told the FBI that the customer who handed him the money was a stocky African-American male, about forty years old with a mustache.

McGuire, Guido, and Doug Ball had done incredible work, but time was running out. The investigation was hitting on all cylinders, but the case hadn't budged at the Nassau County D.A.'s office. Their backs had been against the wall for months. Now they had something tangible to go on. Henry Devine put Ed McCarty on the case full-time. It was time to make a play.

They decided to wiretap Charles Berkley's phone. McCarty then had McGuire send Berkley a loaded letter seeking his "cooperation."

"Mister Charles Berkley, we are requesting that you sit for an interview at the Nassau County District Attorney's Office. New information has come to light concerning your relationship with

Mister Richard Warren Williams, and we may be able to help you avoid serious legal entanglements. Your cooperation is necessary."

They hoped Berkley would read the letter and make a call to Williams, but he didn't. Berkley did nothing but go about his regular business. It was a perfect example of what made the case so frustrating. "These are not your average crooks," an FBI agent was quoted saying in *Newsday*. Williams and Berkley were incredibly disciplined. Williams and Berkley were pros.

McCarty and McGuire were taken aback when Berkley made his own play. He called McGuire and scheduled the interview. McCarty figured one of two things would happen: Berkley would roll on Williams when he dropped the hammer, or Berkley would make a mistake.

McCarty, a junior prosecutor, commandeered the elected district attorney's main office to enhance the perception of power. He sat behind his boss's grand, ornate desk. He may have been young, but McCarty projected authority. He held the keys to Berkley's future, although he wanted Richard Williams.

McGuire met Berkley and escorted him inside the wood-paneled room.

"Hello, Charles," McCarty said straight-faced. "How would you like the deal of a lifetime?"

McCarty then took his time painting a damning picture: Berkley's history with Williams, his knowledge of the Acme Steel Partition profit sharing fund, and the phone calls to Hawthorne, California, prior to my kidnapping. The Ford Mustang, the credit card receipts, the unnamed informant who linked him to Williams—McCarty laid it all out, item-by-item. He wanted Berkley to feel the pressure.

"So, what's it going to be, Charles? I'm prepared to grant you immunity," McCarty said.

Berkley paused, looked McCarty in the eye and said, "I don't know what you're talking about."

In fact, that's all he said. Berkley turned around and walked out. McCarty and McGuire were stunned.

Not only would he go radio-silent, but Berkley disappeared within the week and wouldn't surface again for four years. Police believed his parting gift was to secretly warn Williams. Luckily, Doug Ball had been watching.

On the morning of September 6, 1976, Williams quietly slipped away from Los Angeles in a motor home that pulled an International Harvester TravelAll—a mid-'70s version of the modern SUV.

On the east coast, McGuire was playing a solitary round of golf before heading into the office. Hitting the links helped him think. When he returned to the clubhouse, an urgent message was waiting from the D.A.'s office. "Call ASAP."

McGuire dialed from the club.

"California's moving, Dick. They need to know what to do."

"Follow him!" said McGuire. "Tell them to follow the son of a bitch. Gimme thirty minutes."

McGuire threw on a jacket and raced toward NCPD headquarters in an unmarked car.

It was Labor Day, and by outward appearances Williams was just another highway vacationer. But in truth, he was on the run. He drove along I-15, heading northeast into the desert. The FBI pounced when he stopped in Barstow, a town situated around a road junction about two hours from Los Angeles.

From Barstow, one can continue driving northeast to Las Vegas or cut due east toward Arizona. Authorities believed Williams may have been heading back to New York, but McGuire and Moran wondered whether Williams was planning to take a series of southward backroads that would've led him to Mexico.

Barstow was also the eastern edge of the Los Angeles-based U.S. attorney's jurisdiction, and Doug Ball knew a local magistrate in Barstow who was friendly to the FBI. Williams stopped to service the thirty-two-foot motor home at Barstow Tire & Brake before crossing the Mojave Desert. He went inside a free man and came out in handcuffs.

Richard Warren Williams was arrested at 11 a.m. on Monday, September 6, 1976—almost two years after I was abducted at gunpoint from my driveway. He was at the register when the FBI seized him. Williams gave up without a fight—surprising, given that he had $10,300 in marked one-hundred-dollar bills on him.

A woman and two children were escorted off the motor home while it was searched. Williams refused to identify them, though they were later released back in L.A. He'd been under surveillance for six months as authorities amassed evidence and hunted for alleged kidnapping accomplices. Now, he was in custody.

The motor home was taken to a nearby dealership. An expert from the company examined the vehicle off-site.

"See anything unusual?" Doug Ball asked the man as he walked around looking it up and down. "Look over here. This thing's brand new, and up there by the overhang there's some chipped paint near the screws. See it?"

The serviceman stood on a ladder, removed the screws, pulled on the siding, and one-hundred-dollar bills came raining down. "Jackpot." In all, $20,300 was confiscated: $10,300 from a money belt Williams was wearing and $10,000 hidden in the ceiling of the motor home—all one-hundred-dollar bills, all with matching serial numbers to the ransom money.

The TravelAll was torn apart in an effort to find the rest of the money, but nothing turned up.

Williams was charged with interstate transportation of monies obtained from an unlawful activity—a federal crime.

McGuire flew to California the same day and landed at a nearby Marine Corps reserve center. He then hand delivered a separate arrest warrant charging Williams with my kidnapping. It was New York's victory lap.

"It's a fantastically long and complex story," said Commissioner Guido at a New York City press conference. Guido and J. Wallace LaPrade, the FBI's Assistant Director from the New York Office, identified Richard Williams as the first suspect who was arrested and charged as result of Operation Jacknap.

"Williams was one of many, many names developed over a year ago," Guido said. He also praised McGuire and Moran for their persistence and dedication. LaPrade said the money was identified "by denomination and serial numbers," and that authorities were still searching for other suspects.

LaPrade said they were also trying to determine if there was more unspent ransom money, which was hugely important to me. Another $18,000 was found hidden in a wheel well of the motor home two days later. Where was the rest?

Reporters called me for comment throughout the next few days, but I had no desire to talk. I was elated about the arrest and didn't know Williams. One reporter came to my house. I gave him a few words so he'd leave: "Everyone did a superb job, and there is nothing else I can say."

The next day, Williams was arraigned in federal court and held on a $500,000 bond. He was facing a five-year prison term and a $100,000 fine for extortion and illegal money transportation.

We had to get him out of California. Five years and a fine?

In a sign of what was to come, Williams waived his right to an attorney and claimed to be unemployed. He wasn't cooperating with investigators, either.

"What about this being released on your own recognizance?" he asked the judge assertively.

"That's not possible in your case, Mister Williams," the judge replied.

McCarty was furiously assembling evidence for a grand jury proceeding back in Nassau County. He also obtained an extradition order from a local district court judge that night.

Several days later, a grand jury returned an indictment after hearing seven witnesses over six hours. Williams had been indicted on first-degree kidnapping, first-degree conspiracy, and first-degree grand larceny.

He was going to face justice in New York come hell or high water.

11

The Criminal Trial

Once Richard Warren Williams was indicted, it was a done deal. Or so we thought. He was coming to New York—not that he didn't try to fight it. In fact, he did everything he could to obstruct and delay accountability from that point forward. But prosecutor Ed McCarty and Det. Sgt. Dick McGuire stayed one step ahead.

Williams decided against representing himself once extradition seemed imminent. He accepted a public defender who immediately filed a stay. McCarty wanted to address the Los Angeles court himself but chose to care for his ailing father instead. He sent Deputy D.A. Angelo Delligatti in his place. Delligatti, a longtime confidant, pulled the finest get-outta-Dodge trick I'd ever heard.

During a post-arraignment hearing, Williams's attorney argued for Williams to remain in California. Delligatti had already submitted the extradition paperwork to the judge. Included was New York

Gov. Hugh Carey's signature. Delligatti also obtained a trump card: California Gov. Jerry Brown's signature on an extradition warrant.

"Your Honor, it's my understanding that the governor's approval allows for the defendant to be remanded to the custody of an agent of New York State."

Delligatti was walking a fine line. He was technically correct, but if he pushed too hard his intentions could be interpreted as an arrogant challenge. He was not in Mineola, Long Island, with a familiar county judge. He was in federal court in one of the largest districts in the country.

The presiding judge flipped through the extradition papers and said, "Your documentation is complete."

"Your Honor," replied Delligatti, "I'd like to take custody of the defendant right now."

The judge was nonplussed but agreed to the bold request and ended the hearing. Williams's attorney was enraged.

Williams was escorted from the courtroom. Rather than return to Men's Central Jail, operated by the L.A. County Sheriff's Department, Delligatti had him transferred to the Santa Monica Police Department jail. He knew Williams's attorney would fight and delay. The evening transfer bought enough time to fly Williams to New York early the next morning.

Detectives McGuire and Moran personally accompanied Williams on the journey. Given the distance, a commercial flight was necessary. They left LAX on November 20, 1976—two years to the day that I returned home from the kidnapping. They landed at JFK, mere blocks from where the Keeper released me. I still remember the pungent smell of the black shoe polish he smeared on my face, the phony blind man's cane, and the terror I felt standing blindfolded next to his car as I wondered if I'd feel a bullet hit my back. Now, my captor was on a flight sandwiched between two of my heroes.

It must have been quite the scene. Two Richards, McGuire and Williams, diametrically opposed in their worldviews and chosen paths in life, sitting next to each other as they flew from one great

American coastal city to another. One dedicated two years of his life to the single-minded pursuit of justice on my behalf, while the other tried to evade justice at every turn.

The trio checked in early and boarded separately, per airline regulations. Det. McGuire surrendered his gun, which was stored out of reach in a cockpit lockbox. Federal flight procedures also prohibited Williams, a dangerous criminal suspect, from wearing handcuffs for safety reasons. If anything happened, McGuire and Moran would just have to deal with it.

McGuire sat in the aisle seat. Moran took the window. They crammed Williams in between. He was edgy but didn't talk much. None of them did. He fidgeted, picked his fingernails, and bounced his knees incessantly. He gave off an unsettling vibe. He was passive but difficult. He probably realized he had nothing to lose. But where was he going to go?

Shortly after takeoff, Williams popped up. "Bathroom," he said demandingly. McGuire went with him. It was the first of several "bathrooms."

Upon his return, Williams made a tone-deaf request.

"Can I have a glass of wine?" he asked.

"No, Richard. You can't," McGuire answered incredulously.

Williams's sense of entitlement was obnoxious. His attitude was that other passengers were having drinks and enjoying cocktails, so why couldn't he? Why was he being singled out and denied? The cops were protecting other passengers' affluent leisure while boxing him in and making sure he couldn't partake. They made him watch. It was a slight that cut to his core.

Except, in reality, Williams had been indicted for first-degree kidnapping. He was also caught spending the ransom money. That's why he was on the plane. That's why McGuire didn't buy him a drink. They weren't on vacation. But that context, as stark as it was, was lost on him. In his mind, Williams was the victim.

It would've been easy to berate him, to wish him harm, to knock some sense into him. But McGuire was the consummate professional, a man dedicated to protecting the innocent and upholding the law. Williams was detestable, but McGuire's job wasn't to beat him up. He was a law enforcement officer. Williams was a law breaker. Now, the chase was over. McGuire won. And Williams would face justice in a court of law.

McGuire checked his emotion at the wine request, looked Williams sternly in the eye, and said nothing. To himself, he made it a joke. "If I can't drink, you can't drink."

Williams tested the detectives' patience several more times on the flight before McGuire finally put his foot down. "You're done for today, pal. The next time you get up is when we walk off this plane."

They let every passenger deplane before exiting. Next stop, Nassau County police headquarters.

McGuire and Moran entered the station with the town's most wanted man. It took two years, but they captured the elusive suspect alive. Their peers stood up out of respect; many thought the case was unsolvable.

Williams was booked on conspiracy, grand larceny, and kidnapping. However, trouble started almost immediately.

Richard Williams refused to be fingerprinted. He was uncooperative and rude. At his arraignment, McCarty petitioned the judge to compel Williams to comply with basic booking procedures. The judge declined on the grounds that Williams's defense attorney had asked to be relieved from the case. When he received new counsel, the judge would revisit the issue if it wasn't moot. In the meantime, Williams pled not guilty, and the judge set bail at $1 million.

Williams took his time retaining a second lawyer. Then, he fired him. He also continued to refuse fingerprinting and other basic formalities. Eventually, County Court Judge Alexander Vitale had enough and held Williams in contempt.

"Mister Williams, you are hereby held in contempt of court for refusing to submit to police processing," said Vitale.

Williams's third lawyer was a real gem, Donald Kane. He was uniquely suited to represent his new client, due more to his personality than legal expertise. Kane was an experienced defense attorney who had a malcontent reputation. He was known for spitefully grating the police despite once being a police officer himself. Kane would push the straight-laced McCarty so far at one point, that McCarty restrained himself from punching Kane in the face.

"He called me a coward," said McCarty. "He deserved to get knocked on his ass."

Kane set the tone of his involvement on day one. His first courtroom argument? A pork sandwich.

"Your Honor, it's absolutely outrageous that my client is subjected to a pork sandwich for lunch! Pork is bad for his diet," said Kane.

The outburst occurred during a pretrial hearing eight months after Williams had been held in contempt. It was clearly meant to obstruct the proceedings. Kane reveled in being disliked. He evoked negative responses which he then used to cement his disgruntled views.

His inanity took over the morning court session—and this became a pattern. A representative from the jail had to be summoned to explain on the record that every inmate received the same food and that Richard Williams wasn't singled out.

"It's not a restaurant," the jail administrator said.

Kane wasn't satisfied. Judge Vitale intervened.

"Mister Kane, it is not possible to have food specially made or brought to your client. Perhaps you could buy him a sandwich and the Court could proceed with its business?"

After a lunch recess, Kane continued his antics. He knew the prosecution and the judge would go out of their way to give every benefit of the doubt to the defense to eliminate any controversy surrounding the high-profile case. The evidence would convict. There was no need to taint the trial with shortcuts, innuendo, or tricks. Knowing this, Kane pushed until he forced controversy and then pointed to it to question the fairness of the proceedings.

"Your Honor, I bought my client a sandwich, but the sheriff's deputies wouldn't give it to him," he said on the record. "They said the sandwich was against security regulations."

Williams then stood up and screamed at the judge while con-
tradicting his lawyer. "They tried to give me a lettuce and tomato
sandwich, but they didn't wash their hands!"

"I haven't eaten. I'm too weak to continue," yelled Williams.
"Court adjourned!"

The first pretrial hearing was turning into a fiasco.

Judge Vitale slammed his gavel and pressed on. "Enough, Mister
Kane! That's enough. The Court will proceed with determining evidence admissible for trial."

The hearings lasted months. So did the delays. Williams had
attempted a hunger strike to gain personal privileges and attract
media attention, but quit after several days. He also failed to show
for court one day and claimed to be gravely ill. "I can't continue," he
said, refusing to leave his detention cell.

Williams protested that he had severe stomach cramps and flu-
like symptoms. Judge Vitale ordered a doctor's examination, and the
diagnosis revealed he was fine. "The judge doesn't believe I'm sick, so
I was forced to be here," Williams later blurted out in court. Vitale
banged his gavel and cleared the courtroom. He then launched into
a health discussion with both the defense counsel and prosecution.

"I spoke to the doctor, and I'm satisfied with his opinion. He
said Mister Williams is in good health, or at least good enough to
continue."

"The doctor didn't even lay a hand on him, Judge," Kane
complained.

"A doctor was no closer to me than you are right now!" yelled
Williams from across the room.

Kane quickly interceded. "Your Honor, he's terribly upset and
physically spent. He's suffering terrible conditions. It's wearing him
out," said Kane.

Williams was also causing disruptions in jail. He organized
fellow prisoners, demanded reforms, and inflamed tensions between
inmates and guards. He even sent Judge Vitale a handwritten letter
demanding the charges against him be dropped. "I have been in a

total of five jails relative to this case, for a period exceeding one year under conditions that have caused severe stress and physical deterioration," he wrote. He then accused the FBI and Nassau County Police Department of prejudice and said his right to a fair trial was ruined because of mischaracterizations. "They've called me wealthy, a fugitive, a black militant, and a self-styled revolutionary. I'm none of those things," he wrote.

Kane worked his own angles, including public relations. "My client doesn't fit any of those descriptions," he told the press. "He's a black defendant being tried in predominantly white Nassau County."

Kane tried to postpone the schedule of pretrial hearings on the grounds that law enforcement in the case couldn't be trusted.

"How can we debate admissible evidence if we can't trust the investigators who obtained it, Your Honor? The defense would like to conduct its own investigation. It's the only way we can be sure," he said.

Judge Vitale replied forcefully: "Denied."

Kane then tried another tactic.

"Your Honor, the defense would like the Court to order the district attorney's office to return the defendant's mobile home, diaries, and other personal belongings so they can be sold to raise money," said Kane.

"Mister Kane, I can't authorize that. Those items are evidence," said the judge.

"But the defense cannot investigate ninety percent of this case because of lack of money," said Kane.

While he played games inside Judge Vitale's courtroom, Kane did the same outside of it. He went over the judge's head by petitioning the state supreme court to suspend the proceedings and simultaneously asked an appellate court to grant a change of venue, thereby stripping Vitale of his authority.

Kane wanted the case to be heard in Williams's home borough of Brooklyn, not in the area where my kidnapping first took place, but he was denied both appellate and high court requests.

Every time McCarty introduced evidence—practically every time he spoke—Kane objected. It made for slow progress and sharp exchanges. Kane the instigator, McCarty the counter puncher. At times, the sparring was personal. Kane once heckled McCarty to "sit down."

"Mister Kane, would you please tone down your belligerency this afternoon?" Judge Vitale reprimanded.

"I'm not belligerent, not in the slightest," Kane responded.

The judge called Kane and McCarty to the bench and told them both to cool it. "I'll let you beat up on each other. I don't intend to get involved in your clash of personalities. But I expect a level of decorum."

"Okay," said Kane.

"Yes," said Vitale. "You will say 'Yes,' in this courtroom."

One of the more interesting evidentiary conflicts arose from whether to include a receipt from an African colonel and a book of poetry. Both were found inside Williams's motor home when he was arrested.

The receipt was for a $10,000 donation to the Organization of African Unity, dated March 1975 and signed by a Colonel Hashim Mbita of Tanzania. It was addressed to Richard Warren Williams and mailed to a Jamaican hotel. Thanks to the FBI, McCarty was able to show that Williams's passport confirmed he was in Jamaica from March 9 to March 12.

It was a tight circle of key facts. It also fit with what the Keeper told me in the tenement. "The money is going out of the country...," he said. "The money is going overseas to buy food for poor people... Your people will have to learn not to keep all the money for yourselves...Jew slumlords...Are you in the JDL [Jewish Defense League]... The Jews are going to kill Arafat, aren't they...I'm helping poor blacks and Palestinians..."

"That's not proof of anything!" Kane erupted. He knew the consequences of admitting the evidence at trial.

"That piece of paper doesn't prove a transaction occurred. There's no bank records of any money changing hands, and it's quite improbable such a thing would ever occur. It's far more likely the defendant made it up to be a big shot and show his friends," said Kane.

"The OAU was established for commendable purposes," he continued. "It has a bad reputation because it was headed by Idi Amin. But that has nothing to do with the defendant or the charges brought against him."

Idi Amin, dubbed the "Butcher of Uganda," was a brutal military dictator who ruled the central African country of Uganda with an iron fist from 1971 to 1979. Amin began his military career as a cook and ascended to the rank of Commander of the Army. In 1971, he launched a violent military coup and declared himself president. A year later, Amin broke ties with the West and turned to Muammar Gaddafi of Libya, African dictator Mobutu Sese Seko of Zaire, and the Soviet Union for support.

Amin became chairman of the Organization of African Unity in 1975. In 1976, he allowed Palestinian terrorists to land a hijacked Air France passenger plane at Entebbe Airport, about thirty miles from the Ugandan capital city of Kampala. The hijackers belonged to the Popular Front for the Liberation of Palestine. They took control of the plane after it left Tel Aviv, Israel, en route to Paris. Several more Palestinian terrorists were waiting on the ground at Entebbe to take possession of eighty-three Jews and Israeli citizens. One hundred fifty-six other passengers were released unharmed. A daring Israeli rescue attempt, known as Operation Thunderbolt, freed all but three hostages, who were killed along with seven terrorists and forty-five Ugandan soldiers.

The event occurred just eighteen months prior to that day in Nassau County court and was not unknown by most Jewish Americans.

Historians credit Amin with killing up to five hundred thousand Africans through war, political repression, ethnic cleansing, and human rights abuses. He's considered one of the worst despots in African history and chaired the OAU the same year Williams appeared to donate $10,000. I had been kidnapped less than four months earlier.

The other controversial piece of evidence was a book of poetry titled, *We Just Be Righten*. It overflowed with black militancy and anti-Semitism, as evidenced by poems like "Soliloquy of a Sniper." The book was authored by "Kufanya," a known alias of Williams's.

"So he's anti-Israel," Kane acknowledged. "The defendant's politics are not on trial. Furthermore, his personal views are being treated with such contempt and hostility that it could influence jurors of Jewish persuasion."

"Your Honor, we'd be advancing a kidnapping case into a political trial," said Kane.

The Keeper was clear about why he chose me: I was Jewish, we had money, and he was helping poor Africans and Palestinians. The OAU receipt and the poetry book seemed entirely relevant. They helped establish motive. McCarty had already made Williams's political motivations a pillar of his prosecutorial strategy. He said so in his pretrial opening statement. However, he'd have to think of something else.

After hours of opposing arguments, Judge Vitale ruled against admitting the two items. He also denied the prosecution from introducing any evidence that would connect Williams's political beliefs with those of my kidnappers.

He also ruled against the prosecution's request to compel Williams to provide handwriting and voice samples, which he had refused to supply since his extradition from California in November 1976.

McCarty eventually moved through a mountain of proposed evidence, including twenty-five large exhibits and photographs, and forty witnesses. Kane chose not to disclose his defense strategy; rather, he argued against the credibility of the individuals and items as they were presented by the prosecution.

He unsuccessfully filed for a mistrial, claiming documents pertaining to hypnosis sessions hadn't been handed over to him, but they were virtually useless. It was another distraction. I had paid for the sessions myself.

Then, at the proverbial eleventh hour, Kane pulled another stunt. He asked Judge Vitale to release him from the case.

"Judge, we're presenting our last piece of evidence," implored McCarty. "I estimate two hours and we'll be finished with the entire pretrial process."

"Mister Kane," said Judge Vitale, "on what grounds do you seek relief from your client?"

"My back, Your Honor. The case has become detrimental to my health, and I'm afraid I may need to be hospitalized," Kane said.

Steeling himself, the judge withheld ruling on the motion and instead sought a same-day consultation with Kane's physician. When the hearing resumed, Judge Vitale announced with pained frustration that Kane's request was denied. He wagged his finger at Kane with one hand and waived a stack of papers at him in the other.

"Richard Warren Williams has appeared on the court calendar more than fifty times. This case is going to trial!"

It was now December 1977. More than a year of motions and pretrial hearings had transpired until Judge Vitale finally ordered jury selection to begin. He set a trial date of January 16, but that proved out of reach.

Kane managed other delays. He demanded a three-week postponement after the holiday break so he could begin his own investigation. "Since the Court has declined to appoint a county-financed investigator, the defense will need more time to show that the kidnapping was in fact committed by another man," Kane petitioned.

It was preposterous, and the judge saw it as such. However, in doing so Kane had finally revealed his trial strategy: Williams was framed. The entire case was a conspiracy against Richard Warren Williams. The police, the FBI, his acquaintances, his former employees, his daughter's Mustang, his militant background, and his possession of hundreds of one-hundred-dollar bills with matching serial numbers to the ransom money was all part of a carefully crafted conspiracy. That was Kane's play. And if he needed to stoke racial tensions to his advantage, he would.

The first day of jury selection commenced in early February— not that any jurors were actually selected. Instead, Kane launched into a prepared statement about racism and economic discrimination regarding the historical composition of Nassau County juries. He requested that many more minorities and poor people be added to the jury pool.

"In this county, very, very few blacks get on the panel," he said. "Nassau juries are blue-ribbon!"

Kane also requested that welfare recipients make up a substantial portion of the jury pool, saying, "We don't want a jury of bankers and employees of Grumman, Republic, and Con Edison." Grumman, or Grumman Aircraft Engineering Corporation, which later became the mega-defense contractor, Northrup Grumman, was one of the largest employers in the area.

The entire first day was devoted to addressing Kane's concerns. The county's Commissioner of Jurors testified that prospective jurors are almost always chosen at random from voter rolls, tax assessment rolls, telephone books, and motor vehicle registrations. He also explained that an internal survey showed that 5.9 percent of Nassau County jurors were African American, and data from the county planning commission indicated that African Americans made up 5.6 percent of the county's population at the time.

As a result, Judge Vitale denied Kane's jury pool requests but decided to formally appoint Kane a county-attorney for the defendant. In practical terms, local taxpayers would now pay for Williams's legal bills. Kane would also keep any monies Williams had paid him, and the county would foot the bill for pending and future expenses, such as the $1,000 tab Williams had already incurred for court transcripts. He kept copies of everything to review in his jail cell, though he'd yet to pay for them.

By the end of the first week, the prosecution and defense failed to select a single juror. McCarty and Kane fought vigorously over a panel of 150 prospects, each strategically using their twenty peremptory challenges to eliminate prospective jurors. McCarty had levied six challenges and Kane, five. All but fifteen jurors were excused because they could not afford to participate in what Judge Vitale estimated to be a three-month trial. The judge then asked the county to send more candidates for the coming week.

"Starting Monday, there will be a veritable deluge of jurors to choose from," he announced.

As the peremptory challenges approached the limit for both sides, the selection process drew nearer to conclusion. By the end of the third week, 225 prospective jurors had been called; four were selected. They'd need twelve regular jurors and four alternates for the trial.

The final composition of the jury included a retired school custodian, three self-described housewives, two Grumman employees, a letter carrier, a Social Security office worker, an aircraft mechanic, a plumber, a carpenter, and a truck mechanic. One of the housewives, who sold real estate part-time in the Poconos, was the jury foreman.

Kane immediately asked for the jury to be sequestered for the full length of the trial, but the request was denied.

It all seemed to move so slowly until that point. I'd been kidnapped more than three years earlier. Williams had been arrested one and a half years earlier. I wondered at times whether they'd ever arrest a suspect, and when they did, I wondered whether anything would ever come of it. The pieces all fit, so what was taking so long?

Now, there was no more waiting. The trial would start March 1, 1978, and the first witness to be called was me. I was thirty-five years old. I'd never told anyone outside of Janet and the police what happened. Soon, I'd relive the kidnapping in court for all to see.

Above: Police Photo: Jack Teich's Lincoln in the driveway of his King's Point home where he was kidnapped at gunpoint.

Below: FBI Photo: The vinyl money bag the kidnappers hid in a trashcan and ordered Janet Teich to fill with $750,000.00.

Above: FBI Photo: Janet Teich before the money drop at Penn Station.

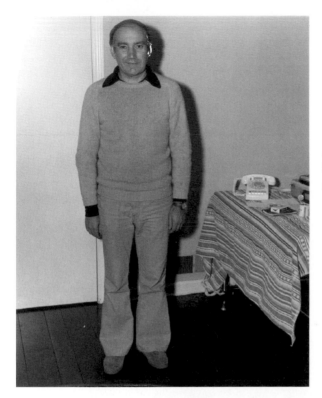

Left: FBI Photo: Buddy Teich, Jack's brother, before the money drop at Penn Station.

Right: FBI Photo: A suspect carries a large bag outside of Penn Station after Janet and Buddy Teich dropped $750,000.00 in a locker near Track 17.

Above: Police Photo: (Left to right): Detective Sergeant Dick McGuire, Assistant District Attorney Ed McCarty, and Detective Jim Moran.

Above: Police Photo: The investigators.

Below: Police Photo: The recovered Mustang the kidnappers used to transport Jack Teich.

Above: Police Photo: Nassau County Police Department financial map tracking the kidnapper's transactions coast-to-coast across America.

(Without Beard)

(Without Beard and Glasses)

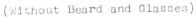

Artist's sketch of an individual being sought by the FBI and the Nassau County PD as a participant in a $750,000 kidnapping.

This person is a black male, approximately 5'9", stocky build, possibly speaking with a West Indian accent.

If you see someone you believe to be this person, take no action. Contact the NY FBI Office (phone: 212/535-7700) or the Nassau County PD (phone: 516/PI6-1111) immediately.

This person may be <u>Armed and Dangerous</u>.

Right: Richard Warren Williams (center) arrested in California, arriving at JFK Airport. Left to right: Nassau County Detective Sergeant Dick McGuire; kidnapper Richard Warren Williams; Detective Jim Moran.

Left: Police schematic sketch of the room Jack Teich was held captive in for a week.

Above: Press photo: Janet, Jack, and Eddie Teich after rescue walking out of NYC FBI headquarters on 69th Street.

Below: Leaving FBI headquarters at five in the morning, Manhattan.

Newsday / THE LONG ISLAND NEWSPAPER

15 CENTS
WEDNESDAY
NOV. 20, 1974

LI Man Is Kidnaped, Freed for $750,000

The week-long abduction of a Kings Point manufacturer kept secret during talks

By Richard Galant and T. J. Collins

New York—A wealthy Kings Point manufacturer who was kidnaped by two men and held prisoner for a week was released unharmed last night after his family paid a $750,000 ransom, the FBI and the Nassau County police announced early today.

The kidnaping was kept secret by authorities. More than 200 Nassau detectives and FBI agents worked on the case as negotiations with the kidnapers were carried on.

In an early morning news conference at FBI head-

A wire service story quoted an FBI spokesman as saying that "there is some indication of political motivation." The wire service, Associated Press, said the spokesman did not elaborate. When they were asked by reporters at the news conference whether Teich was kidnaped by political radicals, Curran and Malone had said they refused to rule out any possibility. They would not comment further on the search for the abductors.

Teich's home in Kings Point is described by local police as modest by Kings Point standards, on an acre

Above: Newsday headline, November 20, 1974

Below: Daily News headline, November 20, 1974.

DAILY NEWS
FINAL
NEW YORK'S PICTURE NEWSPAPER ®
15¢

Vol. 56. No. 127   Copr. 1974 New York News Inc.   New York, N.Y. 10017, Wednesday, November 20, 1974*   Rain, 17-56. Details p. 105

MAN HELD WEEK, FREED FOR 750G

—Story on Page 3

1st Fatal 747 Crash; 152 Die

—Story on page 2

New York Post

Post-O: $2500 Every Week
Game No. 36 • Page 57

AQUEDUCT SCRATCHES / CITY LATE / OVER THE COUNTER.

Pop Scene
WITHOUT ELECTRICITY • Page 65
— Jan Hodenfield • Page 65

Garment Center, N.Y.
By Joyce Purnick • Page 41

WEATHER
Showers, 50s.
Tonight:
Showers, 40s.
Tomorrow:
Cloudy, 40s.
Cloudy Friday.
SUNSET: 4:33
SUNRISE TOMORROW: 6:49

FOUNDED 1801. THE OLDEST CONTINUOUSLY PUBLISHED DAILY IN THE UNITED STATES.

NEW YORK, WEDNESDAY, NOVEMBER 20, 1974
© 1974 The New York Post Corporation

Vol. 174 No. 4

20 Cents

$750G Ransom Frees L.I. Exec

Fare Fight Shifts to The House

By George Arzt

Worried city officials watched the House Rules Committee in Washington closely today as it con... the ... the mass-transit aid bill that is crucial to any hopes of saving the 35-cent fare.

Although the bill glided easily through the Senate yesterday by a 66 to 17 vote, the rules panel presents the most formidable obstacle because of a...

By Dick Brass

Police and the FBI to-day threw 200 men into the search for the ab-ductors of Jack Teich, a wealthy Nassau County businessman who was kidnapped a week ago and held in chains until his release late last night after the payment of a $750,000 ransom.

The kidnapping, which...

examined by a physician early today and pro-nounced in good health. They said he apparently had not been grossly mis-treated during his week-long ordeal.

Edwin Teich said the family was relieved that ... brother was released unharmed. He said the release came a day before...

The investigation is be-ing handled jointly by the FBI and Nassau County detectives. They did not disclose further details of the ransom delivery or Teich's release.

Police said Teich was abducted by two men after he left the offices of the Acme Steel door, par-tition and shelving com...

bers of his family are co-owners of the companies. His wife discovered his car in the driveway of their luxurious home at 2 Ballantine St., Kings Point, at 7:25 p.m. on Nov. 12.

Teich, a father of two, apparently was abducted as he arrived home from work, according to the...

Above: New York Post *headline, November 20, 1974.*

Newsday

THE LONG ISLAND NEWSPAPER

15 CENTS
THURSDAY
NOV. 21, 1974

U.S. Files Antitrust Suit To Break Up Bell System

Trustbusters seek to force the largest firm in the U.S. to sell its manufacturing subsidiary, Western Electric. Page 3.

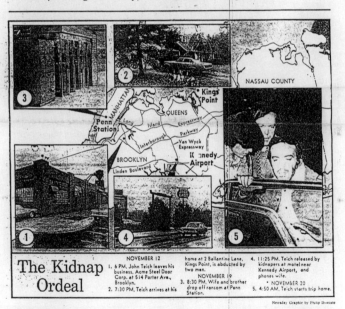

NASSAU COUNTY

Kings Point

MANHATTAN

QUEENS

Penn Station

Long Island Expressway

Interborough Parkway

Van Wyck Expressway

Kennedy Airport

BROOKLYN

Linden Boulevard

The Kidnap Ordeal

NOVEMBER 12
1. 6 PM, John Teich leaves his business, Acme Steel Door Corp. at 514 Porter Ave., Brooklyn.
2. 7:30 PM, Teich arrives at his home at 2 Ballantine Lane, Kings Point, is abducted by two men.

NOVEMBER 19
3. 8:30 PM, Wife and brother drop off ransom at Penn Station.
4. 11:25 PM, Teich released by kidnapers at motel near Kennedy Airport, and phones wife.

NOVEMBER 20
5. 4:50 AM, Teich starts trip home.

Newsday Graphic by Philip D'uosio

Intricate Plan Leaves a Cold Trail

Pages 4-5

Above: Newsday headline, November 21, 1974.

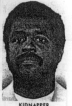

Above: National Enquirer headline, February 21, 1984.

Below: Daily News headline, November 21, 1974.

Kings Point kidnap victim Jack Teich speaks in Nassau court about his abduction and seven days of captivity in 1974. *Newsday Photos / Dick Yarwood*

Suffolk Counts Pennies

In reversal, seeks to keep ¾-cent tax

By Rick Brand
STAFF WRITER

In a topsy-turvy afternoon of politicking, the Suffolk legislature late yesterday voted down a $117-million measure asking Albany to extend a temporary three-quarter-cent sales tax levy only to have a Republican lawmaker do an about-face minutes later to approve the bill.

The tax proposal initially failed in a 9-8 vote with one abstention, despite warnings that losing the revenue would lead to drastic property tax increases and a battering of the county's bond rating on Wall Street.

After the vote, supporters voted to table the proposal until Monday, when the lawmakers plan to meet in a special session on other matters. That led Legis. Paul Tonna (R-Huntington Station) to change his vote, explaining that he will be on vacation Monday and that the sales tax issue is too crucial to delay indefinitely.

"It took a little time to sink in, all the vital programs that would have to be cut," Tonna said. "The county needs the money."

In Suffolk County, the sales tax is 8.25 percent. The three-quarter-cent levy brings in an estimated $120 million a year. The extension expires Dec. 31.

The proposal was initially blocked by six of the seven Democratic legislators in attendance and the three Huntington Republican lawmakers, who wanted the county to seek an extension for only a half-penny sales tax levy.

Legis. Steven Hackeling (R-Asharoken) said he wanted the smaller extension because the legislature earlier this month proposed using a quarter-cent sales tax to pay a $1.2-billion tax judgment for overassessment of the Shoreham nuclear power plant. "I don't care how you spin it," said Hackeling. "We'd be increasing the sales tax, and I don't like that."

He maintained that the legislature could find ways to cut the $40 million needed to keep property taxes in check "instead of giving the money away to Brookhaven."

Tonna's surprise move brought an angry response from other Republican lawmakers, particularly those from Brookhaven, site of the Shoreham plant. "I don't care how you posture and pontificate," said Legis. Joseph Caracappa of Selden. "But this is the height of fiscal irresponsibility."

Legis. Martin Haley (R-Rocky Point) warned that inaction could threaten the county's fiscal health because it is unclear whether state lawmakers, who must authorize the sales tax extension, will meet again after they adjourn around July 4. "If we table it, we'll miss the session," he said.

The sales tax vote came only minutes after the legislature voted down a plan by Legis. Allan Binder (R-East Northport) that would have altered the use of tax revenue to pay the Shoreham judgment so that Long Island Lighting Co. customers in Nassau and Suffolk would get the same electricity rate reductions and would have forced Brookhaven to pay $50 million because the town benefited from overassessing the plant for years.

The county legislature also voted to give county workers an early retirement incentive. Backers say the plan could affect more than 270 county workers and generate savings of up to $8.8 million.

The legislature last night also approved a package giving at least $3.1 million in raises to 400 management employees not covered by union contracts through 2000.

Though the Gaffney administration originally wanted raises of 4 percent in 1996 and 3 percent each year for 1997 to 2000, it settled for cost-of-living increases with a floor of 2 percent annually and a ceiling of 4 percent.

'You Killed Me . . . Not In Body, But in Spirit'

LI kidnap victim talks of '74 ordeal

By Pete Bowles
STAFF WRITER

Facing the man he said abducted him and held him for ransom 23 years ago, Kings Point businessman Jack Teich spoke out for the first time yesterday about his ordeal and the pain it caused him and his family.

"You killed me for seven days, not in body but in spirit and feelings," Teich told Richard Warren Williams. "You made me hate. But fortunately, it gave me the appreciation of life itself and to be free, and love and be close to my family. You can't threaten me anymore, Mr. Williams. You gave me enough pain and suffering over the last 20 years."

Williams, 64, standing before a judge in Nassau County Court in Mineola, smiled several times during Teich's 30-minute delivery but remained silent when he was offered a chance to speak.

As part of a plea-bargain agreement, Judge Frank Gulotta Jr. then sentenced Williams to 6⅔ to 20 years in prison — less than the 20 years and two months he already had spent behind bars for the $750,000 kidnaping in 1974. Williams walked out of court a free man, refusing to speak to reporters.

Williams, who insists he is innocent, was arrested in 1976, convicted in 1978 and sentenced to 25 years to life for kidnaping, grand larceny and conspiracy. His conviction was overturned in 1994 by an appeals court that found that black prospective jurors had been improperly dismissed.

Williams, who was released from jail on $100,000 bail last October, pleaded guilty to reduced kidnaping and conspiracy charges last month. "He has not admitted to anything, but

Richard Warren Williams, convicted in the $750,000 kidnaping, listens.

rather has agreed to . . . [enter the plea] for health and other personal reasons," his attorney, Thomas Liotti, told the judge yesterday.

Liotti told reporters that Williams, described by prosecutors at his trial as a strident black militant, had been framed by FBI agents who Liotti charged planted $38,000 of the ransom money in Williams' motor home before he was

Please see **KIDNAP** on Page A26

Above: Jack Teich delivers his profound Victim Impact Statement in Court. *Newsday*, June 25, 1997.

Below: Forty-five years later—Lifelong Friends: Jack and Janet Teich, Det. Sgt. Dick McGuire, and The Honorable Ed McCarty.

Above: Jack and Janet Teich.

Below: Marc Teich, Lisa Teich, Michael Teich, Jack Teich, Janet Teich, Jaime Entner, Stuart Entner.

The Stand

I had spent the past three and a half years trying to heal. Now it was time to dredge up the pain publicly. It was the last thing I wanted to do, but it was necessary for justice to be served. That was my hope. That's what I told myself as I took the witness stand.

The interested parties, the press, and curious onlookers packed the courtroom. As we waited for the judge to enter, I noticed an empty chair. It was for Charles Berkley. He had been quietly indicted at the same time as Richard Warren Williams, and the indictment had just been unsealed. However, Berkley was nowhere to be found. He was still on the run.

"All rise," announced the bailiff. "Nassau County Court is now in session, the Honorable Judge Alexander Vitale presiding."

I took a long, slow breath and let it out even slower. My moment of truth had arrived.

"Mister McCarty, please call you first witness," said Judge Vitale.

I half-stood as my cue was being delivered.

"Your Honor, at this time the People would most respectfully call Mister Jack Teich," said McCarty.

I immediately felt the concentrated intensity of the room: the stares, the interest, the drama. It affected my gait as I walked to the stand. I had to remind myself to breathe. I just wanted to get started and get it over with.

After swearing in, McCarty began at the beginning. "Mister Teich, on the evening of November 12, 1974..."

His questions allowed me to describe the ordeal.

"It was about 5:30 p.m. when I left the office," I answered. "I was driving a 1971 Lincoln, two-door hardtop. I drove to a stop sign blocks from my house. It was 6:30 p.m. It was the same route I always take. A pair of low headlights pulled behind me. I didn't think anything of it. Five minutes later, I was in my driveway, and the car pulled behind me. Its bright lights pointed in my direction."

"'Excuse me,' I heard a voice say. 'Excuse me, you know how to get to Northern Boulevard?' The voice came from a man wearing a ski mask. He walked toward me with a shiny handgun. Then he pointed it at my head. 'You're coming with us,' he said. I saw another man with a ski mask holding a rifle," I said.

At McCarty's direction, I told of the gas can on the backseat floorboard of the kidnappers' car. "It was inches from my face. I was blindfolded," I said. I explained the cardboard they used to cover me as they instructed me to lay down on the backseat, then the handcuffs, the toll, the bridge, the uphill ride, and the tenement apartment.

I spoke of the Keeper and how he was on a self-imposed mission, "to feed hungry, poor Palestinians and blacks."

"He said one of my captors, the one called Umfudisi, had his wife and children killed by Israelis in a napalm bombing. He said, 'Just so you know how he feels about you,'" I recalled.

"What did that mean, Mister Teich?" asked McCarty.

"That I'm responsible because I'm Jewish," I answered.

I spoke of the closet while the jury of five women and seven men listened. I explained I was kept in the closet for three days until I was "promoted" to a metal-frame bed.

"They put chains around my arms and legs and fastened them through eye hooks at opposite ends of the closet. They ran a chain around my neck," I continued.

"How big was the closet, Mister Teich," asked McCarty.

"Maybe five-feet by two-feet."

"Did they ever untie you? How did you use the restroom?"

"No," I answered. "They gave me a bucket. I laid prone for three days and figured out how to maneuver within the small bit of slack."

"What happened next?" asked McCarty.

"They moved me to a metal bed in the middle of the room."

"Could you see?" asked McCarty.

"No, I was also blindfolded and made to wear taped-over glasses. He also kept the lights off the entire time."

McCarty continued until introducing the ransom tapes. Kane tried to suppress them during pretrial evidentiary hearing but failed. He knew how damaging they'd be when heard by a jury of everyday people. Kane protested again to no avail. Then demanded the judge clear the courtroom.

"Publicity is preventing the defendant from receiving a fair trial!" he implored.

Judge Vitale called both Kane and McCarty to the bench and conducted a whispered discussion. He then denied the defense counsel's motion. It was a win for our side, but I took absolutely no pleasure hearing those tapes. They were haunting.

McCarty pressed play. Anguished, tortured voices filled the courtroom.

"Hello."

"Janet?"

"Yes."

"If you want to see him again, it's seven hundred and fifty thousand dollars. We will call you tomorrow."

"Wait! What?"

"Seven hundred and fifty thousand dollars. You will be called tomorrow."

I had never heard that before and never wanted to hear it again. The terror in Janet's voice was too much. It was indescribably wrong. *Why? For what?* There was no good reason for any of this. I was reliving the emotions of the kidnapping all over again.

McCarty played more tapes.

"Hello."

"Janet there?"

"Yes. This is Janet."

"Tell Buddy to go to the Exxon Station..."

"Wait! Wait, please. Is Jack—"

"Tell Buddy—"

"No, please! I can't remember. Is Jack ok?"

"Stop talking and listen!"

"Can I speak to Jack? Is he alright? Where is he?"

The tape continued before ending in a loud dial tone. It hung in the air amid stunned silence. A feeling of collective shame came over the courtroom.

McCarty played a third tape. This time it was Buddy.

"Is my brother alive? Please tell me. I have the money, but I must have proof that he is alive. I have the money...You can have the money. I've got three-quarters of a million dollars, but I want my brother...."

"I will call you at the phone booth behind the New York Information Booth at 6:30," the kidnapper said.

"Behind the New York Information Booth? Will you prove to me then that my brother is alive? When will I have proof? I will have the money with me. Three-quarters of a million dollars. It's everything I've got. You can have it...."

The human anguish was disturbing. Hands rose to cover mouths; people shifted in their seats. I shivered with disgust. Meanwhile, Kane attempted to draw attention away from the tapes. He made frustrated gestures and intimated he couldn't hear what was being said. He squinted, looked toward the ceiling, and shook his head side-to-side. The voice opposite Janet and Buddy was not as clear, and Kane used it to his advantage.

"Objection!" he said. "The audio is unclear, and there is no proof that is the voice of the defendant!"

"Overruled," said Judge Vitale.

Next came a tape with my voice. I told how I was forced to record it in the darkness of the tenement before McCarty pressed play. "I'm in a place where there is no escape from. The group is serious, and they mean what they say. Janet, don't call the police. They don't want any deceit. They'll know if the money is marked, and they'll know if there are any bugs. I've told them about the family, and they have the names and addresses of everybody."

Buddy would tell of finding the tape in a gas station trash can later in the trial. It was placed in a trash bag along with the black ransom bag, some personal items of mine proving the kidnappers had taken me, and a message from them: "Pay his fine of $750,000, or he will be executed. If your corrupt police get involved and make attempts to trap us, Jack will die. Then the entire family becomes targets. You are being watched...Death to fascist capitalists."

It was awful. All of it. Absolutely awful. But paradoxically, that helped us. The trial was off to a good start. It was far from over, but we'd won the first day.

That evening, Kane filed for a change of venue and told the press that if the motion was received favorably, then he would move for a dismissal on double jeopardy grounds since the trial had already started. I often think about that day when I hear people clamor for their proverbial "day in court." It's not all it's cracked up to be, even when it goes well.

* * *

I TOLD MORE OF MY STORY THE NEXT DAY. It was cathartic on one level, traumatic on another. McCarty was honest and steady. He drew straight lines while Kane took the substantive, evidence-driven narratives and threw them into the air like a stack of papers to force McCarty try to pick up the pieces and try again.

"The man you said held the pistol in your driveway," said Kane. "You said he was short and plump. That's what you told the FBI, is it not? You said he was five-foot-five, isn't that correct?"

"I was shaken up pretty bad when I first spoke to the—"

"Yes or no, Mister Teich."

"Yes," I said.

"But you told Mister McCarty in this courtroom that he was five-foot-seven. Correct?"

"Yes," I said.

"We can all plainly see that the defendant is five-foot-seven. He's also quite trim—but that's beside the point," said Kane. "There's a big difference, Judge, between five feet, five inches and five feet, seven inches," Kane said with courtroom flair.

"Objection," said McCarty. "The heights are not inconsistent, Your Honor. Mister Teich was a victim of an unimaginably horrific event. He offered his best estimate of the main kidnapper's height after he was rescued and was off by two inches. Two inches!"

"Overruled," said Judge Vitale.

"Thank you, Your Honor," said Kane. "The bigger problem here, ladies and gentlemen of the jury, is that Mister Teich told the FBI one thing and with Mister Williams in the courtroom, he's saying another. I'm not sure why."

"Mister Teich," he continued, "I'd like to go back to the night you were abducted from your driveway. Were you familiar with whether an area on your way home called Steamboat Road was primarily a section settled by black people?"

"Steamboat Road? Yes, I guess so," I said. I had no idea where he was going, but it was clear he was racializing the case.

"And that's on Kings Point, correct?"

"Correct," I said.

"Okay. As you came home that evening and as you pulled into your driveway, looking at People's 2 in Evidence, or the map of the area, as you were pulling into your driveway, was it black...or dark?" asked Kane.

"I don't understand," I said.

"There were no lights on. That's what you told the FBI. You said there were no outside lights on, and the headlights of the kidnapper's car silhouetted the masked men and caused you to squint," said Kane.

"Objection, Your Honor," said McCarty.

"I'll rephrase," said Kane. "During your debriefing you told the FBI that your kidnappers 'must have been black.' I'll repeat: you said they 'must have been black.' That's not a definitive statement, is it Mister Teich?"

"I don't understand," I said.

"You didn't see your kidnappers that night in your driveway, did you Mister Teich? In fact, you never saw them, did you? You told the FBI the main kidnapper wore gloves. You told the FBI they wore ski masks. You said the only time you caught a glimpse of them was in a dark room, and that you only saw the lower part of a trench coat. Isn't that correct, Mister Teich?"

"I had just been released when they debriefed me and—"

"Yes or no, Mister Teich. Yes. Or. No. I've restated facts from your debriefing immediately after you were taken to FBI headquarters. This occurred within an hour or so since you last had contact with them. Wouldn't that be the best time to explain what happened? When your recollection was closest to the actual events? I'm simply restating your own words," said Kane.

"By the way, can you identify the defendant's voice as the voice of one of your kidnappers? I remind you, you are under oath," he continued.

"Not with absolute certainty," I said.

"Okay. Now, this is important. Did you ever at any point see the face of the one you call the Keeper? And did you ever see the faces of any of your kidnappers?" Kane asked.

"No. No I did not."

"That is all, Your Honor," said Kane.

The exchange was brutal. Kane was a son of a bitch, but he was skilled. He made me the bad guy and Williams the victim.

But I did get a little satisfaction at the end of two long days on the stand. Kane had a copy of my grand jury testimony, and, of course, he had a copy of my post-release FBI debrief interview. McCarty decided to have a go at twisting the knife in Kane's back for once and asked the judge to have the defense return the photocopied items since I had finished testifying.

"Your Honor, it's imperative that the defense relinquish these materials on the grounds that another man, one closely associated with the defendant, has been indicted for Mister Teich's kidnapping and has not yet been apprehended. Mister Charles Berkley is a fugitive from justice who could clearly benefit from the information contained therein," said McCarty.

Judge Vitale ruminated before deciding to grant the request. Kane was incensed. But before he could object, Williams was shouting at the bench from his chair. "Remove yourself! Remove yourself if you can't be fair!"

The judge slammed his gavel. "That's enough from the defense table," he admonished.

Kane demanded to keep the copies. He argued his defense strategy would be hopelessly lost without the transcripts, which was ridiculous. What Kane really wanted was an on-the-record fight to cast aspersions on the trial.

"Judge, I've made notes in the margins that would reveal my innermost thoughts to the prosecution," he said. "I don't know how we could continue."

"I see," said Vitale, nodding. "Let's have a compromise."

The judge ordered his assistant to tear up the papers in open court. That way there could be no speculation about Kane's notes reaching the prosecution, and no chance of Williams passing sealed grand jury testimony or details of my FBI interview to Berkley or anyone else.

Shwww shwww shwww. It was delicious. The long, slow *riiiiipp-ping* of page after page of Kane's personal copies of the transcripts was deeply satisfying. The bailiff held up sheets of paper to demonstrate his thoroughness. His objection was an obvious ploy that blew up in his face. He tried to look busy and unaffected, but the sound was inescapable. His visage morphed into a purple rumpled prune as his lips puckered with bitterness. He feigned writing on a yellow legal pad to pass the moment. It was the first time I smiled in days.

Williams couldn't take it, either. He boiled with anger. He'd racked up thousands of dollars in transcript fees that he had no intention of paying—indeed, the county ended up paying for them—and he fully expected to get his own copies of the documents. He was entitled to them, or so he thought.

"Do you have some good reason not to let me share with my attorney something that means my life?" Williams shouted.

"Sit down, Mister Williams! That is enough!" said Judge Vitale, his patience exhausted.

* * *

IN THE PROCEEDING WEEKS, McCarty called dozens of witnesses and steadily built a tower of evidence against the defense. Kane took calculated shots at the cornerstones.

Janet testified next. McCarty played the tortured ransom tapes again for her and then later for Buddy. I sat through them each time. It didn't get easier. In fact, it was harder because I had to bury my rage while the defense attacked my wife and brother.

Then, McCarty moved to other witnesses and evidence, such as Eugene Hardeman. He was a Jacksonville, Florida plant store owner who testified that he saw Charles Berkley and Richard Warren Williams together in the northeast Florida city in winter 1975. The eye witness account was the first to connect the two men after my kidnapping.

Hardeman said Williams moved three doors down from his longtime residence, and that he helped Williams install a new fence, shed, and roof at his house. Hardeman also made interior remodeling repairs, he explained.

"Are you absolutely sure that the defendant is the same man you remember helping?" asked McCarty.

"I'm positive," said Hardeman.

"And you're sure that Charles Berkley was with him?"

"I'm sure," he said.

"How are you so sure?" asked McCarty.

"Because my family was the only black family in that neighborhood for at least ten years until Mister Williams moved in," he said. "We were happy the neighborhood was growing in that respect. We got to know each other as I helped him fix up his house."

"Is there anything else you remember about the defendant?"

"Yes. He moved his mother in, and he liked to be called an African name, Kufanya," Hardeman said.

Kane leaped at the chance to cross-examine the witness. He attacked Hardeman's credibility by asking him things he couldn't remember, like the address of the police academy he attended more than a decade earlier.

"How can you recall casual details about Mister Williams and not more important, more involved events in your life?" asked Kane.

The questioning grew personal. Kane asked about intimate details of Hardeman's children and then skewered him when he couldn't answer. Kane kept Hardeman on the stand for two days. He took a seek-and-destroy approach designed to erase the witness's factual contribution to the case in the minds of the jury. Kane became so aggressive that McCarty eventually objected on the grounds that he was "battering" Hardeman.

"Sustained," Judge Vitale said.

McCarty then called Keith Gordon to testify. Gordon was a Florida mobile home salesman who attested to selling Richard Williams the mobile home he was arrested in. He said Williams made a cash payment of $20,000 in one-hundred-dollar bills.

"He took the money from a black gym bag," said Gordon. "He even gave me five one-hundred-dollar bills as a tip."

The money was deposited in a local bank, but the serial numbers on the bills were never compared with the ransom money. The deposit occurred a year and a half before the FBI was aware of the transaction, and bank officials said the bills had long been distributed.

"Did he identify himself as Richard Williams?" asked McCarty.

"No. He said his name was James Washington."

"Was he accompanied by anyone else?" asked McCarty.

"Yes. A taller man who walked with a limp. He sort of dragged his foot when he walked," said Gordon.

Just like one of the kidnappers! I thought.

"Did the defendant say anything else that stuck out in your mind?"

"Yes. After he gave me the five-hundred-dollar tip, he asked if I could recommend a real estate agent. He said he had some money to invest, and he wanted to buy some land in Florida."

It was devastating testimony. But when Gordon said that Williams financed $10,000 of the mobile home cost by having a friend named Ford—who lived in the area—take out a bank loan, Kane pounced.

"Isn't it possible that the twenty-thousand-dollar cash payment was made by Mister Williams on behalf of the Fords? The one-hundred-dollar bills could've been the Fords' money, right? You can't say otherwise with one hundred percent certainty, can you?" said Kane.

"No," said Gordon.

In truth, the FBI and Nassau County police detectives had suspected Ford was privy to the kidnapping, perhaps directly involved, but they couldn't prove it. Real estate would've been a plausible way to launder the ransom money, as well.

Kane tried to destroy Gordon by suggesting he was dishonest and that he pocketed the $500 he called a tip, when it was really meant to pay for service repairs on the mobile home.

"How is it that your company received the money, but you didn't give Mister Williams a receipt?" Kane asked. "Didn't you leave your company soon after?"

"Yes," said Gordon, "but that has nothing to do with the twenty thousand dollars or...Washington or Williams or...or his mobile home."

Kane let Gordon's defensiveness hang in the air before retiring.

"No further questions, Your Honor," he said.

McCarty then called a California supermarket cashier to the stand, Edward P. Yorke. He described the customer who paid him with a one-hundred-dollar bill as African American, stocky, short, and about forty years old with a mustache.

"Do you see the customer in the courtroom?" asked McCarty.

"Yes," said Yorke. "He's sitting at the defense table."

The cashier then told how the FBI entered the store shortly after the exchange and confiscated the bill, which turned out to match a ransom bill. The testimony appeared another win for the prosecution.

McCarty called other witnesses who gave equally damaging testimony, including Williams's Los Angeles landlord and a service repairman who both received one-hundred-dollar bills with matching serial numbers from Williams. McCarty called FBI agent Doug Ball to the stand, who personally recovered the bills, to explain.

On cross examination, Kane ripped into Ball. He would be ground zero for Kane's conspiracy theory defense. "Why didn't you save your notes, Agent Ball? You're supposed to keep all records and items relating an arrest, correct?"

"Yes," said Ball.

"So why did you get rid of your handwritten notes about Richard Williams? Why him? What was it about him?" said Kane.

"I threw them away after I included them in an official report," said Ball.

"How are we supposed to know if those notes were relayed accurately?" said Kane. "You could have made a mistake, and nobody would ever know. You wouldn't leave anything out or misconstrue information on purpose. I know you wouldn't do that. Everybody knows that. It could never happen in the rush to make a high-profile arrest."

"Objection!" shouted McCarty.

"I'll reframe," said Kane. "Look, those aren't the only notes missing, are they Agent Ball? In fact, you destroyed notes from six—SIX—witness interviews in connection with this case."

Kane thrust six fingers in Ball's direction and held them up for effect as he panned toward the jury.

"Did you even bother to fingerprint the bills in question when you obtained them?" asked Kane, already knowing the answer.

"Fingerprint the bills? No," said Ball.

Then Kane not-so-subtly suggested that Ball was a major figure in a subversive investigation. He painted a dark picture with sinister hues and said the FBI did an extremely poor job on the case from the ransom money drop at Penn Station all the way to Williams's arrest. The Bureau needed to save face so they arrested an African-American, he implied.

Kane kept Ball on the stand for six days. He tried to break him. McCarty fought relentlessly to keep Kane in check. Judge Vitale excoriated both attorneys for wasting the Court's time.

"Three hundred and forty-two pages," said Vitale. "Three hundred and forty-two pages. That's the amount of testimony for this witness," he said regarding Agent Doug Ball. "And forty-five to fifty percent of this is talk between the lawyers and the Court!"

Kane seized on the reprimand. He blamed the delays on McCarty's objections and then on the judge himself for sustaining them. It was clear Kane had ulterior motives. He was angling for a mistrial. We were seven-weeks into the three-month trial, and Kane had asked Judge Vitale 250 times to grant a mistrial. Two hundred and fifty times he was denied.

All the while, evidence piled higher and higher against his client. A California businessman testified that the voice on the ransom tape was without question his former business associate, Richard Williams. The Ford Mustang discovered from gas station credit card receipts that were signed by James Washington, a.k.a. Richard Williams, and registered to Williams's daughter, Celestyne Williams-Glen, was one of only two such vehicles that had chrome trim around the windows—something I told the FBI in my post-kidnapping debrief. The Mustang was sold not long after my kidnapping but was found by Nassau County police detectives. They searched it and found a strand of hair that forensic lab tests later confirmed was mine. Williams Burrell, Jr., chairman of the Pan-African Studies Department of San Fernando Valley College, testified that he hired Williams as a part-time teacher in 1969. Burrell, Jr. appeared as a character witness for Williams, but when asked if Williams ever went by the name "Kufanya," he said proudly, "of course he did." That admission, however, opened the door for a book of anti-Semitic, militant poetry authored by Kufanya to be entered into evidence. Judge Vitale also allowed McCarty to enter the Organization of African Union receipt into evidence that was addressed to Williams and reflected an amount of $10,000 he paid in cash in March 1975. Vitale denied the receipt letter during pretrial hearings but allowed it after FBI agent Thomas O'Quinn testified to finding it in Williams's mobile home in Barstow, California. O'Quinn independently corroborated my earlier testimony that the Keeper vowed to send the ransom money out of the country.

The hits kept coming, and Kane kept acting out in desperation—as did Williams.

Williams socked a jail guard in the eye on the way to court one day. The altercation occurred during a routine inspection of his case files. Paper clips and other items are supposed to be removed for safety reasons, but Williams took issue without warning. He was restrained by two other guards and suffered a sprained wrist. The affair was handled administratively, not criminally, and caused a delay in the trial proceedings.

Kane invented his own delays and constantly pushed for recesses. He seized on hypnosis transcripts that he hadn't received from the prosecution during discovery. These were transcripts from private hypnosis sessions that I paid for, but they were the perfect foil for Kane's pseudo quest for a fair trial.

"Your Honor, this case reeks to high heaven," he said. "The misconduct perpetrated by the prosecution has created a cloud over this case. The prosecution has hid documents and refuses to allow the defense grand jury testimony and seven hours of FBI interview transcripts taken immediately after Mister Teich was released. The defense demands a mistrial!"

"Your Honor," said McCarty. "The prosecution has turned over everything the law requires us to do. There is no basis for a mistrial."

Judge Vitale cleared the courtroom. Nine days later, he announced his decision.

The Verdict

I honestly didn't know what was going to happen. I knew the right man was on trial, but I didn't know anything about technical hangups or procedural violations. It was all up to the judge. He waited two calendar weeks to rule on Kane's best shot at achieving a mistrial.

"Mister Kane, I take your calls for mistrial very seriously," said Judge Vitale.

"I agree in some respects that the production of hypnosis documents should have been more forthcoming to the defense. Mister Teich was not required to produce them, but to the extent the FBI was aware or participated, the government is required to produce them. I understand you've now received transcripts and that you have obtained them through subpoena," said the judge.

"I've considered your request for mistrial on the basis that you would have questioned Mister Teich differently if you had said documents prior to his testimony. I have closely reviewed these same documents as they relate to Mister Teich and to what has transpired over the past ten weeks of this trial. I have put myself in your shoes, Counselor. I've been on both sides of the adversarial relationship in our system of justice, and I have performed honorably as an appointed judge overseeing that relationship for some time. I have explored the issue at hand from top to bottom, and I have concluded that there is no indication of bad faith, as you allege, on the part of the prosecution that would warrant a mistrial," Vitale said.

"Furthermore, I have reviewed your intermediate motions. First, your motion to dismiss the charges against the defendant is denied. Your request for the county to pay the travel expenses for defense witnesses, six of whom have arrived or will arrive from California, is denied. Your motion to poll jurors to ascertain whether they've read or heard a *Newsday* report outlining inadmissible evidence regarding the political aspects of this case is granted. Your request to declare a mistrial if any single juror has been exposed to such information will be taken into consideration. Your request for the Court to appoint your law partner as a county-paid defense attorney is granted. Your request for a one-week recess to prepare your defense in light of the hypnosis transcripts is granted. And I will also allow for the defense to recall eight prosecution witnesses, including Mister Jack Teich," the judge continued.

"But Judge, if I knew what I know now, I would have cross-examined all the witnesses differently," said Kane.

Despite the gravity of Judge Vitale's commitment to resolving Kane's ploys, Kane continued his effort to derail the trial. It was naïve to think he'd snap out of it if the judge gave him what he wanted. The court gave the defense more time, money, and flexibility to better make their case, but Kane wasn't satisfied. Williams wasn't either. He wanted the charges dropped. "You are perpetuating this trial under the guise of professional dignity when it really is diabolical treachery!" Williams yelled.

Judge Vitale ignored him.

A week later, the judge held a special hearing for Dr. Herbert Spiegel without the jury present. Spiegel was the psychiatrist and Columbia University professor who conducted my hypnosis session nearly four years earlier. Kane wanted Judge Vitale to admit a tape of the session into evidence because he thought it would damage my credibility. It was actually the first time a New York state court dealt with such an issue.

The judge allowed it, but it didn't change the bottom line.

"Mister Teich had very limited recall of what happened because he was blindfolded," Spiegel later said in front of the jury. "The trance session didn't work because he is not susceptible to hypnosis. The degree of success with hypnosis depends on the subject's personality and biological makeup. I felt sorry for him because there was nothing new to go on," he said.

After nineteen months in jail and fourteen weeks at trial, Richard Williams finally got his opportunity to tell his side of the story. Defendants are not required to testify because it leaves them open to cross-examination, but Williams marched confidently to the stand as Kane called him in dramatic fashion.

The courtroom was packed. News reporters and activists crammed next to witnesses, law enforcement, and members of my family. This was the man they'd come to see.

At Kane's direction, Williams talked about his life—growing up in Brooklyn, Needles Trade School, and California.

"Why did you move to California?" asked Kane.

"Opportunity," said Williams.

"I thought it would be different. It was, and it wasn't," he said. "I became a successful real estate dealer in Southern California helping blacks and Chicanos move into white neighborhoods. They were locked out. I let them in."

"But I couldn't just stand by and take the money," he continued.

Williams said everything changed when he got involved in the education system. "I defended black students during racial demonstrations at San Fernando Valley College," he said.

"Is that when the police started targeting you?" ask Kane.

"Yes."

Williams testified that he was arrested for helping students fight against racial discrimination, but it's at least as true that he was arrested for assaulting a police officer. He called it "persecution."

Williams talked about being a bona fide leader in his community at the time. He was vice president of a local chamber of commerce and held other relatively influential positions in addition to being a successful real estate entrepreneur. Then his business floundered. He blamed the FBI.

"Two FBI agents told me at the time that I was 'a fortunate black man,' because I handled Veterans Administration mortgage foreclosures in my real estate business," he said.

"Meaning what?" asked Kane.

"Meaning they were targeting me for my politics, but my saving grace was that I helped veterans. I told them I objected to their relating my economic life and my personal life," said Williams.

"Rumors spread that I was a supporter of militant activities," he continued. "Banks I had enjoyed good relationships with were denying me credit. There were unsolved robberies at my home and office."

He gestured scare quotes when he said "robberies," insinuating police were involved.

"Why did you leave the United States, Mister Williams?" asked Kane.

"Because I was frustrated. Too many racial problems and nobody doing anything about it. So, I walked away. I had no desire to raise my children here. They shouldn't have to fight to get an education," he said.

One-by-one, Kane brought up the evidence. One-by-one, Williams knocked them down. An Exxon credit card receipt in Larchmont, New York, near my brother Buddy's house? Coincidence. The ransom note in the gas station trash bag? Not him. Williams's former business associate, Aldrich Motley, who testified that Williams's voice was the voice on the ransom tape? Revenge for an air charter business gone bad. Calls with Charles Berkley prior to my kidnapping? Normal chit-chat.

"Did you know Jack Teich before you were arrested?"

"Never heard of him," said Williams.

"Did these telephone calls with Mister Berkley relate to the kidnapping of Jack Teich?" asked Kane.

"Definitely not," Williams replied.

"How do you explain the ransom money in your mobile home?" asked Kane.

Glaring at the prosecution table, Williams said, "*Someone* broke into my mobile home the night before I was arrested. I knew because the electronic burglar alarm was switched off. I kept fifteen thousand dollars, mostly in one-hundred-dollar bills, in a secret compartment," Williams explained.

The inference was that the FBI broke into the mobile home and switched his money with money matching the ransom serial numbers.

"What about the rest of the money? Where did that come from?" asked Kane.

Williams said his shoulder bag contained thousands of dollars from a successful trip to Las Vegas. He said he kept thousands more in the same bag that came from an advance on his "Liberation" board game.

"Was there any other reason why you had so much cash on hand?" asked Kane.

"Yes. I got involved in a gambling operation in Harlem, 1973. I won fifty thousand dollars," Williams said.

He then looked at the jury and described his arrest at Barstow Tire & Brake. "The FBI pointed guns at my children. My fifteen-year-old daughter and eleven-year-old son were running back and forth hysterically. I begged them to allow me to go over and speak to my children, but they ignored me."

Williams spoke in soft, deliberative tones. He was compelling, and a bit seductive. He had an answer for everything, and I worried he might be winning over the jury. Williams's tone changed, however, when Judge Vitale cleared the jury box before denying a defense exhibit into evidence.

"You should be sitting in the D.A.'s chair!" he shouted.

Things got testy when McCarty cross-examined Williams. He'd worked for almost three years to finally confront Williams in court. McCarty was prepared and earnest. Williams was uncooperative and sarcastic. Like Kane, he tried to push McCarty into reacting emotionally. McCarty couldn't take the bait. He knew the defense would point to any reaction as an indication of ill motives.

"Mister Williams, you testified that your mobile home was broken into the night before you were arrested, but you didn't say you checked your money. Why not? Wouldn't you check to see if tens of thousands of dollars were stolen after a break in?" asked McCarty.

"What do you think?" Williams retorted.

McCarty moved to the ransom bag, but Williams interrupted to say the Florida mobile home salesman lied. "I bought a mobile home from him, and I paid the twenty-thousand-dollar price with one-hundred-dollar bills. I *didn't* have a gym bag full of money with me. That's nonsense. Try to do better," he said.

McCarty pressed on, and Williams fired back. "I did not carry such a bag, and I don't believe you believe that yourself," he said, bitterly.

Another flareup occurred when Kane introduced a board game into evidence. It was created by Williams and called "Liberation." McCarty couldn't believe his luck. He seemed surprised, even delighted.

A prototype had been found in Williams's mobile home. He was in the process of marketing samples of the game when he was arrested. Kane wanted to show that Williams was misunderstood. He wasn't a radical but an intellectual who creatively channeled his social insights into an entrepreneurial game.

As he questioned Williams, McCarty realized Kane omitted the game's "almanac," or question booklet. He told an assistant to fetch a copy from investigation materials.

"Objection," McCarty said. "The defense has not entered the whole game in evidence."

After much arguing, Kane was forced to admit the booklet came with the board game. Kane wanted to assuage fears of Williams's militancy, but he opened the door for McCarty to confirm them.

As soon as he asked Williams about certain game questions, Kane roared in opposition.

"Objection!" said Kane. "His political views are not on trial."

"It would be a grave injustice for anyone to read my views from that book," Williams said out of order. "The material in the book reflects my research."

"Quiet, Mister Williams," said Judge Vitale. "You may proceed, Mister McCarty."

McCarty recited from the game booklet: "Israel plays a watchdog role in African affairs, when it is not involved in direct military action. Many Israeli bombs have fallen on African villages in the name of 'coup.'"

"Does that sound familiar, Mister Williams?" McCarty asked.

"No."

"That's the answer to game question one hundred and one. The topic is how Israel is involved in Africa," McCarty explained. He continued with several more questions and reminded the court that I had testified that the Keeper made similar remarks when I was chained in the tenement apartment.

Williams didn't answer except to say that, "Liberation is more than a game. It's an education for children."

McCarty later asked Williams about the $10,000 receipt from the Organization for African Unity. Kane vigorously objected. "Your Honor, the prosecution is intentionally trying to politicize the witness. Mister McCarty knows his questions are inflammatory and prejudicial."

"Overruled," said the judge.

McCarty continued, but Williams denied everything.

"I don't know about a donation. I've never met Colonel Hashim Mbita. I've never been to Tanzania," he said, adding, "I don't know any ambassadors who arrange meetings like that."

McCarty reversed course and reentered with questions that had documented answers.

"Were you in Jamaica in March 1975? Were you staying at the hotel where the receipt was addressed? Were you at the hotel on the day the letter was dated," asked McCarty.

"Then how did you have the receipt in your possession when you were arrested in September 1976," asked McCarty.

"I had seen the receipt, but I don't know who sent it. I just liked it," Williams said.

McCarty decided to challenge Williams. How much would he admit if given enough rope to hang himself? McCarty asked Williams directly whether he thought the FBI planted the ransom money in his mobile home.

"Objection!" shouted Kane. "He doesn't have to take a position. He's here to testify not characterize."

"Sustained," said Judge Vitale. "Careful Mister McCarty. You will ask the question differently or not at all."

McCarty backed in the question, "Mister Williams, did any member of your family, or any friends, place the money there?"

Williams looked at Judge Vitale. "Am I obligated to answer facetious questions about my family in this court?"

"You may answer the question," said Judge Vitale.

After a resentful pause, Williams responded, "Not to my knowledge."

He would testify for two weeks.

* * *

KANE CALLED ME BACK TO THE STAND as his final witness. He actually called me to testify two other times after the judge allowed him to recall witnesses following his subpoena for documents. He milked the extra latitude for everything it was worth.

He wanted to know why I told the FBI that the kidnappers' car was blue with a light-colored top, when I said earlier in court that I didn't remember.

"Again, that was right after I was released. I hadn't seen my family yet. I hadn't slept. It seemed right at the time," I offered.

"Well, it's another example of saying one thing to the FBI and another in front of the jury, isn't it," said Kane. "By the way, do you know what color Mister Williams's daughter's car was?"

"No," I said.

"It's green," said Kane.

"You also told the FBI that the kidnappers asked if you were Jewish after you were abducted, correct?" he asked.

"Yes."

"Then if they didn't know whether you were Jewish, how in the world could your religion have been a motive for your kidnapping?"

"I don't know," I said.

"You told the FBI that you thought you were being robbed and that you were being taken to a—and I'm quoting you—a 'black environment.' Correct?"

"Yes, but I was telling the FBI what the kidnappers told me. I didn't make it up," I said.

Kane's line of questioning attacked my integrity. He portrayed me as someone who would blame an innocent person because of their background. I know he was an attorney fighting for his client, but the approach was still despicable. It made me sick.

The character attack also set up his closing summation.

"Not one person has gotten on the witness stand and physically identified Richard Warren Williams as being a kidnapper of Jack Teich," he said. "Not one."

"The FBI bungled this case at the railroad station. They goofed. They made a colossal error in this case. Nobody thought to test the radio transmitters underground at Pennsylvania Station before the ransom exchange. Can you imagine not knowing that radio com-munications might be affected underground, and with steel girders lining the ceiling and iron tracks all around? There were hundreds of law enforcement officers there to catch one man. A man they saw open a locker, take out a bag of money, and walk to a subway plat-form. But they blew it. The kidnapper got away," said Kane, with an incredulous expression.

"The case is too important, too high-profile, for the FBI to admit their mistake," he continued. "They needed an arrest. So they found a patsy, a scapegoat, a good candidate to take the fall. That's Mister Williams," Kane said.

Kane's surface strategy was to depict a brutal conspiracy against an innocent man. The culprits were the corrupt justice system and cooperating victim, he suggested. "Sure, Jack Teich was kidnapped. But not by Richard Williams."

His real strategy, however, was to cause chaos. His aim was to undermine the trial.

It's not customary to raise objections during closing arguments, but Kane's behavior left the prosecution no choice. He forced their hand.

McCarty issued sharp objections and accused Kane of "injecting himself into the case." Kane responded by blasting the prosecution for using "smart aleck" tactics. Kane then called the prosecution's law enforcement witnesses "antagonistic" towards Williams and said, "The FBI certainly are capable of dirty tricks." Kane told the jury that the testimony of the prosecution's thirty-seven witnesses was of "no signif-icance" because the case hinged on the credibility of law enforcement.

Rather than accuse the FBI outright of planting evidence, he walked through each instance where McCarty had connected Wil-liams to me or the ransom, and showed how the FBI *could* have framed Williams.

"I'm not accusing anyone," said Kane, "but there was certainly the opportunity for someone to place a hair from Mister Teich into Mister Williams's daughter's old car. And somehow that money got into that police stationhouse," he said, referring to the additional $18,000 that was found hidden in a wheel well of Williams's motor home two days after he was arrested.

Kane suggested that I had been "brainwashed" and that I "rationalized to myself that the defendant's daughter's car must be the car of the kidnapper."

"There is reasonable doubt on all three counts, and I would ask you to find the defendant innocent," he finally said. Kane's closing summation lasted nearly six hours, after which he asked for a three-day recess. Judge Vitale said the trial was already a month longer than expected and that he was inclined to continue.

"After four months of trial, I think it is ludicrous to expect me to be prodded and pushed like an animal. I'm exhausted, Judge. I can't take it," Kane said.

"Is that giving me a fair trial, when I see my attorney exhausted!" shouted Williams.

"Enough!" said Judge Vitale.

He cleared the courtroom except for the press. The jury had heard all the evidence, and the prosecution and defense had both made their cases over the sixteen-week trial period. Now, as the jury prepared to deliberate, Judge Vitale dealt with Donald Kane.

"This Court has withstood months of verbal attacks from the defense. Mister Kane, your strong behavior is unparalleled in my experience," said the judge.

"You asked the Court for a recess so you could petition the Appellate Division to send an observer to sit in on this trial. The implication being that the Court was incapable of conducting a fair process. You've directed many remarks at this bench, some within hearing of the jury, that were designed to raise a cloud of uncertainty," he continued.

"Are you familiar with *People vs. Gonzalez*, Mister Kane?" asked Vitale, staring daggers into the defense counsel. "It's a 1975 decision by the Court of Appeals. In *Gonzalez*, the court ruled that a defendant could not claim that he did not receive a fair trial if the defense attorney—I'm now reading a section from that decision, Mister Kane—if the defense attorney 'engaged in tactics designed to disrupt and to infuriate through trial and summation.'

"That is what you have done throughout the past four months. You've made more than three hundred requests for mistrial," said Vitale.

He said his comments were intended to clear the air ahead of the jury verdict and that he had every intention of remaining silent but changed his mind after Kane made a motion for mistrial during his closing. That motion, said Judge Vitale, came at "a grave place in the trial."

The judge wanted it known that he endured Kane's attacks and Williams's outbursts with dignity. "You attempted to provoke the Court, Mister Kane, and the Court would not take the bait. I will make a record later," he said.

"You're making a record now, Judge," Kane retorted.

"Anything I said was not addressed to the bench on a personal basis. Whatever I've said is on behalf of my client," said Kane.

"Mister Kane, during the course of the trial I was impressed with your skill and reputation. However, your comments require this Court to exhibit a strength and firmness and decisiveness commensurate with yours."

* * *

THE JURY WAS SEQUESTERED at a nearby motel after deliberations continued past the first day. The jury forewoman, Millicent LaMarca, told Judge Vitale that the jurors wanted to hear the tapes of the three ransom calls again, and that they wanted to examine the three one-hundred-dollar bills that Williams allegedly spent in Los Angeles stores, which ultimately led to his arrest.

The trial is still one of the longest in Nassau County history. After seventeen weeks, forty-three witnesses, and 123 pieces of evidence, the jury returned a verdict. They deliberated for two days.

GUILTY.

Guilty on all three counts. Eight men and four women said "guilty" thirty-six times for the crimes of kidnapping, conspiracy, and grand larceny.

Kane shook his head and pouted. Williams smirked. "Guilty, guilty, guilty..." He showed no remorse.

"The verdict is consistent with the evidence," said Judge Vitale.

Williams now faced twenty-five years to life in prison. Kane asked that the sentencing be scheduled as soon as possible, then grasped Williams's hand, turned, and left the courtroom. He said nothing to the press except that he would appeal.

McCarty was elated. He announced through a bouquet of microphones that it was "a good day for justice." "But this conviction is only the first phase. This case will not be over until Charles Berkley and the other kidnappers are brought to trial, and the ransom money is returned to the Teich family."

Det. Sgt. McGuire was also in attendance. He was relieved.

"It's a great feeling to know that the work you put in can turn out this way," he said. "It was a long hard road, and I gained a lot of experience. My wife is more relieved the case is over than I am," he said with a smile.

"She had to put up with a lot during the case. Raising kids, running the house, and putting up with my moods when things got sticky." Then, his smile faded. "There are still blanks in the case. Where's the rest of the money? Where are the other kidnappers? Where was Teich held during those seven days he was held for ransom?"

LaMarca, the jury forewoman, told the press that she was taken with Williams. "He seemed very nice, a brilliant man," she said. "It's a shame he didn't use his gifts to be an honest man."

She and several other jurors said that the quality of the ransom tapes was too poor to match Williams's voice. They could hear his voice on tape and in the courtroom, and they couldn't decide whether they were same. Several other jurors, however, believed it was his voice, she said. LaMarca added that every jury member thought it was unlikely that the FBI planted $38,000 of ransom money in Williams's mobile home.

McCarty assured the jury after the verdict that they had convicted the right man. He wasn't allowed to introduce it during the trial, but thanks to the diligence of the FBI and an intercession from the U.S. State Department, a Tanzanian general attested by cable that he had the one-hundred-dollar bills that Williams donated to the Organization of African Unity. He confirmed the serial numbers matched a list of numbers provided by U.S. law enforcement.

McCarty also criticized the OAU for not sending a representative to testify during the trial. Months later, the general returned the full $10,000.

I wasn't there for the verdict. I didn't want to be the center of attention. If Williams was found not guilty, everyone would look to me for my reaction. If he was found guilty, they'd still swarm me. Instead, the prosecution team called me. I was thrilled with what I heard. Absolutely elated.

I prepared a brief statement for the media: "I want to thank the Nassau County police, the district attorney, and the FBI. They did an outstanding, excellent, superb job. I hope the verdict will serve as a deterrent to crime because there is just so much suffering for victims and their families."

I just wanted it to be over. All of it. And for a long while it was. Until Williams got out.

The Technicality

On July 12, 1978, Richard Warren Williams was sentenced to a term of twenty-five years to life in prison for my kidnapping. He received another fifteen years for first-degree conspiracy, and fifteen years more for first-degree grand larceny. Williams was the Keeper, the mastermind behind the horror. Now, he had to pay for his actions—not that he saw it that way. Williams's parting remarks were wholly consistent with the hateful, victim ideology he spewed in the tenement apartment years earlier.

"Given the morality of the FBI and the Nassau County Police Department, and the mentality of this court and an all-black jury, I could have convicted any one of you of the same crime," he said. "The real criminals in this case are those who used their powers and position against me!"

Defense attorney Donald Kane doubled-down on the charade. "The conduct of this court and the tactics of the district attorney deprived the defendant of a fair trial. This trial was a mockery and a miscarriage of justice. I move that the Court set aside the verdict," he said.

"Those are the remarks of a skillful advocate attempting to create a record. The verdict stands," said Judge Alexander Vitale.

"We will most certainly appeal," said Kane.

Moments later, Williams was escorted from the courtroom by a group of uniformed police officers and bailiffs. Several armed attendants stood watch as Williams exited. Next stop: Sing Sing Correctional Facility in Ossining, New York.

Janet, Buddy, and I were relieved Williams was locked away where he couldn't exact revenge on us or hurt anyone else. But to be honest, we still didn't feel safe. How could we? We'd never be the same again. Nobody would. We'd have to learn to live with the experience and do the best we could to manage. Plus, we knew Williams had underworld connections, and the other kidnappers were still at large. Anything could happen at any time.

I tried to move on, but it seemed like there was always something to remind me of the ordeal, like Rudy Williams, Richard Williams's brother. He was the break in the investigation. Actually, Det. Sgt. McGuire broke the investigation by breaking Rudy Williams. After his brother's sentencing, he tried to collect the $20,000 reward Janet and I had set up for information leading to the capture and conviction of the kidnappers, and the return of the ransom money.

Rudy Williams sent two handwritten letters claiming his right and intention to collect the money. *The nerve*, I thought. Hounding us for money when we are missing more than $700,000? My attorneys denied his requests on the basis that the reward conditions hadn't been met. Sadly, Rudy Williams and his son were later murdered. The crime remains unsolved to this day, though McGuire believes their execution-style deaths were due to Rudy's gambling debts.

In April 1980, Charles Berkley turned himself in. He'd been missing since Ed McCarty's surprise interview at the district attorney's office in August 1976. McCarty had offered Berkley immunity in exchange for his cooperation. Instead, Berkley denied everything, walked out of the building, tipped off Williams, and disappeared.

Berkley was the inside man. We employed him at Acme Steel Partition for fifteen years. He knew about the company's robust employee sharing fund because he cashed out when he left the company to open a real estate business. He was an industrial draftsman and had no known background in real estate. That was Williams's expertise.

Months later he joined a competitor's firm and was attempting to be rehired at Acme Steel Partition when I was abducted.

Berkley called a New York television reporter, Felipe Luciano of WNBC-TV, and said he was tired of being on the run, and he was ready to turn himself in. Why not walk into the police station? Why Luciano?

It was another ploy. The kidnappers were smart, no doubt about it. Careful, strategic, and smart.

Luciano helped fashion the public narrative. "He knew about my history of being involved in politics and having been an ex-con. He felt I would understand," Luciano said in a television exclusive.

They met on a street corner in Harlem. Luciano then escorted Berkley to FBI headquarters in midtown Manhattan for dramatic effect. Berkley said in the televised interview that he ran away because he was afraid he would be treated unfairly because of his politics. "I was frightened and upset, but now I think I can deal with it because I have always been innocent," Berkley said.

Worse than the lies was the thought of enduring another trial. *Here we go again.* Williams's trial almost killed me, literally. I had a heart attack—my first one—at thirty-eight years old. The prolonged, unrelenting stress of the kidnapping and the subsequent trial broke me. Janet suffered immensely, too. We wanted our life back, but the truth was that the life we knew before the kidnapping was gone forever. This was our life now.

Berkley was jailed. Det. Sgt. McGuire personally escorted him. Bail was set at $500,000. The district attorney's office sailed through grand jury proceedings and successfully obtained an indictment. They geared for trial, excited for another high-profile conviction. I wanted justice, of course, but all the hubbub meant I would have to relive the trauma again under intense scrutiny.

Berkley was charged with the same felonies as Richard Williams: kidnapping, conspiracy, and grand larceny, all in the first degree. He pled not guilty.

Six months later, the presiding Nassau County Court judge dropped a bombshell. There wasn't enough evidence to support the D.A.'s allegations, he said. Berkley got off. His county-appointed lawyer told the press the judge was "courageous." Standing together on courthouse steps, Berkley smiled and said he was in a state of shock. "I've never felt better," he declared to a gaggle of reporters.

I was numb when I heard. The prosecution was stunned. A spokesman for the D.A.'s office said the court ruling was a shocking surprise, and that renewed investigative efforts would bring additional evidence to warrant a new indictment. But it never came.

Once again, the press swarmed for reactions, and Janet and I faded from public life. We were reminded of our vulnerabilities. Richard Williams was angry and in prison, Charles Berkley was free, and the other kidnappers were unknown and out there somewhere. We lived with these thoughts in the back of our minds at all times.

During that period, we won a civil suit against Richard Williams. Any time he received money, a portion was to be garnished and remitted to my family as restitution for the missing ransom money. This was an ongoing saga that would tie us together for years to come.

Williams used his time in prison to file lawsuits against the prison system and advance his criminal appeals. He was the quintessential jailhouse lawyer. In 1984, he received a settlement of $11,000 for alleged civil rights violations. They amounted to a delayed magazine subscription, an unmet glasses prescription, and exposure to secondhand smoke from other inmates.

How he managed a settlement, I have no idea. It was a testament to his cunning intellect. But there was no way we were going to allow him to indulge the proceeds—not without a fight. Of the total amount awarded to Williams, $5,682.80 was paid directly to the Nassau County Sheriff's Department and the U.S. Marshals Service for administrative expenses incurred at his 1978 trial. An additional $4,964.27 was earmarked for his attorney.

We decided to enforce the civil judgement against Williams's settlement but not for the law enforcement reimbursement—just his lawyer's fee. After some quibbling, we won. Williams received $352.93 and a bill for $5,000 from his attorney. It was a small victory, astronomically short of our due, but it was satisfying.

* * *

AS THE YEARS TICKED BY, Williams became less and less relevant to my life. He was becoming a distant memory. I lived with Williams the Keeper daily, haunting me beneath my conscious mind and occasionally breaking through to torment me. But Williams was less a concern—that is, until his great jailhouse triumph.

In 1986, the U.S. Supreme Court ruled in a case called *Batson v. Kentucky* that prosecutorial peremptory challenges, or the ability of a prosecutor to exclude prospective jurors during the jury selection process, could not be used if the sole reason in doing so was the person's race. I had no earthly idea of the decision at the time, and if you had asked me, I'd have probably said it was a wonderful development. But the way the ruling played out with respect to my convicted kidnapper was less than wonderful. It was dispiriting.

A confluence of events helped Williams weaponize an appeal. First, a fire engulfed decades of court documents at a county storage facility. Among them were boxes of records pertaining to his trial. The fire abetted his incessant legal wranglings by incinerating the jury selection files. It was then determined that the Supreme Court ruling could apply to both past and pending cases. That was Williams's trigger. McCarty, by then a judge, would have to account for why he dismissed six black prospective jurors from a jury pool of more than 200 individuals fifteen years ago if Williams was to remain behind bars.

McCarty remembered why he dismissed three of the potential jurors, but he could not remember why he dismissed the other three. He could've made something up. He could've lied. He could've advanced his interests, and if information to the contrary surfaced, he could've said something lawyerly. But that's not McCarty. He did what he thought was the moral thing to do. He told the absolute truth.

McCarty then called McGuire, who was retired from the NCPD. "We're going to have a problem. They're going to overturn the Teich kidnapping conviction," he said.

"Unbelievable," said McGuire.

In 1994, the Appellate Division of the State Supreme Court upheld Williams's appeal, saying his trial was unfair because the prosecution failed to show that the exclusion of three black jurors was not racially motivated. To be clear, the court didn't say McCarty's actions were racially motivated but that he couldn't show they weren't.

It was frustrating beyond words. Williams found a technical loophole.

On November 8, 1996, Richard Williams walked out of Green Haven Correctional Facility a free man. He was portrayed as a victim, a role he relished—as if he'd been caged for a crime he didn't commit. Bullshit. The press peppered me for comment. I didn't respond.

Despite the celebratory optics, Williams was still in trouble. In overturning his conviction, the appellate court effectively ordered a new trial. He'd been released from custody on $100,000 bail and then moved in with his sister. *Where'd the money come from?* I wondered.

When asked if he'd seek a plea arrangement to avoid trial, Williams said, "I am open to a humanistic approach from the district attorney, and I am interested in being exonerated."

A spokesman for the district attorney's office fired back. "We plan on relitigating the matter. The overturning of this conviction had nothing to do with the evidence in this case. The case remains strong."

The original court files were gone, but the ransom bills Williams had passed to Los Angeles stores were collecting dust in a Nassau County property bureau along with other evidentiary items. McCarty thought there was enough to go on. He wanted to relitigate.

"I'll do it, Ed. I'll go through a trial again," said McGuire.

They were sincere, but both men knew a new trial was unlikely. The case had cost over a million dollars. It would've taken two to three times that amount to do it again. And to do what, exactly? Prosecute a sixty-three-year-old graying man with health problems who'd already served nineteen years behind bars? Good luck getting original witnesses back to court, too. All that aggravation and notoriety? Few public-facing officials would have the stomach for it. But we could push them.

McCarty called me. "Jack, do you want to go through this again?"

"You're damn right!" I said.

Janet and I would've gone to the mat for McCarty, McGuire, the FBI, and the D.A.—all of them. But it wasn't that easy. The emotion of going through another trial would be unimaginable. The first one almost killed me. Did I want to go through it again as an older man? Was it worth exposing my children? Marc and Michael weren't cognizant for the first trial. My brilliant and beautiful daughter, Jaime, wasn't yet born. Now, they were adults. They'd experience the pain and evil brought upon their father—as would their own families. Janet wasn't up for it. How far was I willing to let Williams reach into my life? Generations? What if after all the expense and trouble, the D.A. lost?

A plea deal would spare my family. They are who I thought about in the deepest, darkest hours of my captivity in the tenement. They're the reason I didn't dart into the woods behind my house when the Keeper approached me in the driveway. While I was chained in the closet like an animal, abused, neglected, and abused some more, I thought of them.

I made my decision. I would protect them again and face Williams in court. I'd accept a plea as long as I'd have an opportunity to stand up and confront him within the confines of the law.

* * *

JUNE 24, 1997. It was a warm summer day, not yet hot in the season. Janet, my children, and I were dressed professionally and in good spirits. It was difficult, no doubt. But today was the day I'd been waiting for since my release. An outside observer might guess we were heading to a funeral and making the best of it. Maybe it was a funeral of sorts. The old Jack, the fearful Jack, was giving way to the Jack who had found his voice—the one that was taken by the sadism and greed of the Keeper. Today, with my family's support, was the day I would confront Richard Warren Williams. It took a long time, but I was ready.

"Do the people wish to be heard?" announced a clerk for Nassau County Court Judge Frank Gulotta.

"Yes, Your Honor," said McCarty. "The victim in this case, Jack Teich, wishes to make a statement to the Court at this time."

This was my time. My moment. Not to perform, but to look the Keeper in the eyes and confront him with the truth—something he feared.

"Mister Teich?" said the clerk.

I planned for this. I spent hours upon hours preparing what I was about to say. Each minute invested seem to conjure emotional distress that impacted the here-and-now. It's why so many victims bury the past, because dealing with it plunges them back into the trauma no matter how much time has passed. But you can't move on unless you relive the pain and confront its source.

The clicking of my shoes on the courtroom floor echoed as I approached a podium. It reminded me of the intensity of when I took the witness stand long ago. I cleared my throat, took a deep breath, and looked at my papers. *I can do this. Just get started....*

"I would like to thank the Court today for allowing me to speak," I began.

I then turned and faced the Keeper.

"Mister Richard Warren Williams, alias Mister Charles R. Lee, alias Mister James R. Washington, alias Mister Kufanya, I am here today to confront you and to speak out, which I could not do in 1974 or during your trial in 1978," I said. "Kidnapping and extortion is a vicious, horrendous, cowardly crime because it has more than one victim; my family, my wife, my children, my deceased father, the rest of my family, and all my employees who thought I would never return and prayed for me. The grief and anguish you put our family through is indescribable.

"During the months before you abducted me, you tried to abduct another brother of mine, on two previous occasions, by luring him to remote places, but you failed. We had a prior employee of ours for seventeen years who was a boyhood friend of yours and schoolmate of yours who gave you information about me, my company, my brothers.

"You failed, so you then came to my home when I arrived home from work one evening and at gun point, you forced me into your car, along with an accomplice with a shotgun. You had a pistol, remember Mister Williams?"

I kept going.

"You drove me for about thirty to forty minutes, apparently to the Bronx, where you brought me to a room. You put me into a closet and chained my legs to one side of the closet and my hands to the other side, like an animal, for a week. You then tortured and terrified my family, and did not call them for thirty-six hours to let them know that you had abducted me and that I was alive. I, myself, during this time did not know whether I was going to live or die.

"You then finally called my home and terrorized my wife. This is you talking, Mister Williams, your voice was identified by numerous witnesses at your trial—"

The first ransom tape played.

"You then constantly threatened my life. You then constantly threatened my family's life if they didn't do exactly what you said. You interrogated me for that week, terrorizing me with a gun and forcing me to give you more and more information. You forced me to make taped messages, which you sent to my family. You took pictures of me, which you sent to my family, to extort as much as you can. You constantly made anti-Semitic statements and rhetoric to me throughout the week. You constantly made anti-white statements and rhetoric to me throughout the week.

"You then terrorized my wife and my family again and called my home a second time. I will play this tape, the second call, to refresh your memory, Mister Williams. You will also remember your voice was identified by numerous witnesses at your trial and by myself. You then demanded by extortion seven hundred and fifty thousand dollars in cash from my family."

The second tape played. He squirmed as sounds of abuse and agony filled the courtroom. My family sat still and somber.

It was all coming out, now. Momentum took over. I felt stronger and stronger.

"You killed me for seven days, not in body, but in spirit and feelings. You made me feel helpless. You made me hate. But fortunately, it gave me the appreciation of life itself, and to be free, and love and be close to my family. You can't threaten me anymore, Mister Williams, or is it Mister Charles R. Lee, or Mister James R. Washington, or Mister Kufanya? You gave enough pain and suffering over the last twenty years.

"You then called my home again and talked to my brother, Buddy, this time to collect your extorted money from us."

The third tape played.

"This again is your voice, recognized by all those who have heard it. You will also remember your voice was identified by numerous witnesses at your trial.

"You made my wife and family suffer waiting to see if I were alive or dead, and if I were alive, what condition I was in. The stresses were so great because of your actions, our family, including myself, sustained direct stress-related illnesses over years because of this crime and your actions. However, with great hardship, we managed to overcome the scars of what you did, and we are stronger today.

"Our family is very close, but this crime has affected each of us in a different way. The stress of the kidnapping, the investigation, and the trial has affected all of my children. They are still very frightened, even today. We were always a trusting family, and I was always a trusting person. We live a much different life today because of your actions.

"Then, during the payoff of the ransom money in Penn Station, you will remember that again you threatened my family with death and threatened me during this last day until you received the money. Then, after you received the money, Mister Williams, you were observed by the authorities, both the FBI and Nassau County police, picking up the money and fleeing into the New York City subway, a moving New York City subway train. You then made my family wait over six hours in agony, and one of your accomplices lectured, threatened me about speaking or telling anything to the authorities, or you would come back and kill our family. You then dumped me like a dead animal on a secluded road near Kennedy Airport.

"Mister Williams, or is it Mister Lee, or is it Mister Washington, or is it Mister Kufanya, you are full of hate and terror. You took what did not belong to you. You terrorized my family, and you have not taken any responsibility for your actions. There is no remorse here today. You have not given up your accomplices in this crime, you have not returned any of the money, you have not taken responsibility for your actions. You actually feel good about what you've done.

"I'm sure you know your brother, Rudy Williams, aided police in the investigation and final apprehension of you in California. After your conviction, your brother, Rudy Williams, and his son, your nephew, were found bound and tied execution style and shot three times in the head in Greenburgh, New York, in Westchester County. This crime has never been solved, and this is still an open investigation.

"You, Mister Williams, may have beaten the system under a technicality, but the Appellate Division found your guilt to have been established. However, you got out of prison before your sentence was up. You think you were so smart and have beat the system. However, don't think you're going home today to celebrate. Today marks a new day in our relationship, Mister Williams, Mister Washington, Mister Lee, or Mister Kufanya, which started in November 1974.

"At the time of your arrest in California, trying to flee to Mexico, you'll remember that you had thirty-eight thousand dollars of my money in documented bills with you. Now you owe me seven hundred and twelve thousand dollars plus interest. Even if I recoup any money, the money will never compensate for the agony that you put me through and my family endured.

"The criminal phase of this case, this crime, will never end in my memory, and I hope yours. However, we still have civil remedies under the law to pursue. We have an active New York State civil judgement against you which now, including interest, is over two million dollars. We will vigorously pursue exercising this judgement to the fullest extent that the law and civil court allows for the rest of your life and your estate after you pass on. Any money you have hidden, any assets or property you may have acquired, any job you may take, any investment you may have made, any accomplices who are holding my money for you, we'll be there.

"Mister Williams, you have not worked in over twenty years. How are you paying for your legal fees? You have paid legal fees previously, and you are still incurring fees. I promise you we'll get to the source of your ability to pay these legal fees. We'll be watching and attach those funds that you owe me. The civil court will find the source of these funds. Whether you are Mister Richard Williams, Mister Charles R. Lee, Mister James R. Washington, or Mister Kufanya, or any other name you select, maybe even Sergeant Muldoon of the New York City Police Department, or Mister Larry Garrett of the U.S. State Department, the names that you used when you attempted to abduct someone else in our family.

"I also understand you intend to sue the Nassau County Medical Center after they treated you at county expense. This sounds typical of what you would do. Rest assured, Mister Williams, if you sue and if you prevail, you will never see that money. We'll attach it, just as we attached your frivolous lawsuit a number of years ago to Nassau County. You didn't see that money then, and you won't see that money now.

"Upon leaving the Court today Mister Williams, you, your wife, your daughter, your sister, your brother, will all be served with subpoenas for depositions in the civil action in exercising our judgements. Rest assured, the Civil Court will find out where the money is harbored.

"I can't end this chapter in my life without, on behalf of myself and my entire family, thanking the so many people and individuals that were involved with this case and my family and myself over the years. The Nassau County Police Department, the FBI, the Nassau County District Attorney's Office, they were all, through the years, the most compassionate to myself and my family as victims. They were also the most professional, intelligent, dedicated, caring, and persistent group of professionals I have ever met. However, they were all persistent for two years until they arrested you in California trying to flee to Mexico, brought you back to Nassau County for trial, and ultimately, conviction. I owe all my thanks and gratitude to those professionals.

"Thank you."

And with that, I sat down. I finished what he started.

"The Court thanks you for coming forward today, Mister Teich. The Court's sympathy goes out to you and your family for what you and yours have endured as a result of this incident," said Judge Gulotta.

There was no applause, no movie cameras, no awards—nothing like that. I simply sat next to Janet, and we held hands. I took a deep breath. I did it. Satisfaction filled my soul as I felt my family's pain and pride.

Williams's trial attorney was nowhere to be found. His new attorney, however, took a page from Kane's playbook and attacked the system that delivered justice.

"Today the case of People versus Richard Warren Williams is drawn to a close, finding its way, at long last, into the history of our criminal law. Yet, the anguish, cruelty, and racism that it has spawned do not end. They linger today filling this courtroom and spilling out of it with uncertainties, questions, and accusations which never end, even if there were a trial here, and irrespective of its outcome."

The judge then announced the terms of the deal. Williams agreed to plea nolo contendere, or no contest, to the original charges. In doing so, he accepted his conviction but without admitting guilt. "He has not admitted to anything," his lawyer reminded everyone within earshot, "but rather has agreed to its entry for health and other personal reasons."

The court clerk asked if Williams wanted to speak. He gave a single word response, his only utterance in the entire proceeding: "No."

The judge read through several formalities before warning Williams that if he made any contact in any form with Janet, Buddy, or me, or our families, then he'd face new charges and die in prison.

That was it. We left and went our separate ways.

As I approached my car, a court officer ran towards me. "Jack! Jack. Wait. Jack!" *Oh no, what now,* I thought.

"Jack," he said. "I just have to tell you. I was the court officer...I was the court officer during your trial twenty-two years ago. I was there. I sat through those four months, and I felt so terrible for you. I just want you to know how happy I am for you today."

The officer reached out and embraced me.

The Missing Money

Another twenty years from that landmark day have passed. Janet and I are much older now. Our emotional lives have been largely restored, though we could never be the same.

When I grew up, I never had a house key. There was no need because we never locked our doors. There was never an issue with losing car keys, either, because we always left them in the ignition.

After the kidnapping, I became much more vigilant. That's one way we changed. We're careful. We lock everything. If I walk across the street, I lock the door behind me. If we're home, I twist the dead-bolts. We lock our cars inside our closed garage. Our home also has a top-line security system complete with emergency panic buttons at every exit.

I keep the office locked at all times as well, and long ago installed a number of surveillance cameras that run live feeds from outside entryways, the parking lot, and around the building. I still check the rearview mirror at traffic lights and stop signs, as if the kidnappers might pull up behind me again. I can't help but alternate my route home from work. As for cars, we buy quality vehicles but nothing too flashy that might grab unwanted attention. Same with so-called "vanity license plates"—they're just asking for trouble.

Oh, and don't even think of buying "kidnapping insurance;" you're advertising to be kidnapped. Your name and the amount of insurance gets seen not just by your broker but throughout the insurance company underwriting the policy. Bad move.

As for work, all my employees now undergo thorough and detailed background tests.

Bottom line: we don't feel safe, and I doubt we ever will. It's sad, but that's the way it is.

One thing I refused to do, however, was to retreat from people who were different from me. That's not safety; that's something else, and I won't accept it. Our housekeeper, handyman, personal book-keeper, and many others who come in and out of our home happen to be from different racial and ethnic backgrounds, religions, and creeds. Some have been with us for decades, and I consider them friends.

Being portrayed as someone with discriminatory motives was one of the worst parts of the ordeal, post-release. It deeply upsets me. I was raised to treat people the same no matter their color or race. There are good people and bad people, and it has nothing to do with their immutable personal qualities. I raised my own children with those values. Yet, I often found myself in a brewing cauldron of racial tension during Williams's trial and then again after his suc-cessful appeal. McCarty and McGuire did, too. It's a shame.

We've had many people come and go at Acme Steel Partition. At the height of our business, we employed six hundred individuals. We treated everyone equally and with respect. In all those years since my father started the company, we were never once sued or cited for discrimination. It's not who we are; it's not what we stand for.

Rarely did we have bad apples at Acme Steel Partition. Charles Berkley was not the norm. We had good, loyal, upstanding people in our company—many of whom had been with us for a long time. My secretary has been with the company for thirty-five years. There have been so many nice, wonderful people that I'm just extremely grateful to all of them.

* * *

THE MISSING RANSOM MONEY IS STILL A MYSTERY.

The kidnapping case never came full-circle because the money was never found, and the other kidnappers escaped justice. To this day, Det. Sgt. McGuire views the case of the missing money as unsolvable. Given his "never quit" spirit, that's saying something.

It always struck me that Williams never cooperated. He could never logically explain the ransom bills in his possession. That was the death knell of his criminal defense. His attorney, Donald Kane, had to know he'd never get out from under it. The FBI stopped him in California days after Charles Berkley went missing. Williams was on the run, agents found thousands of dollars in matching ransom bills in his possession, and he'd hidden thousands more in the wheel well of the mobile home.

A promise to return the rest of the money would have been the perfect bargaining chip in a plea negotiation. Why didn't Williams give it up and walk away with a vastly reduced prison sentence?

He sat behind bars for years appealing his conviction and suing Nassau County and the New York state prison system. He clearly wanted out. He was serving twenty-five years to life, meaning he wouldn't have been eligible for parole until he'd served a minimum of twenty-five years. Yet, he never turned state's evidence. As far as I can tell, he never even thought about it. The D.A.'s office approached him years into the term and offered leniency if he'd give up the money, but he wouldn't budge.

Williams also refused to talk about Charles Berkley or their accomplices. They never rolled on each other. I wondered why. Were they true believers in their militant cause? I never thought so. I'm sure they believed some of what they said, but the anti-imperialist, anti-Semitic hate was really just camouflage for a brutal extortion plot. That's what I think.

My kidnapping was mostly about money, not politics. That may have been part of their motive—a kind of justification for their despicable actions—but at the end of the day, they wanted money. And lots of it. They wanted to be rich. Williams himself was a capitalist real estate entrepreneur who lost his shirt in a failed business venture in South America. He came back to the U.S. complaining about the socialist government of Guyana. Rather than rebuild his business, Williams tried to steal from mine.

As much as he screamed about it, my being Jewish had nothing to do with his greed—envy maybe, but not his greed. He was a coward. The abuse was deeply personal, but it boils down to a crime of convenience.

I don't think we'll ever find out where the money is.

Charles Berkley died several years ago. Richard Williams died more recently. We know because we hired a forensic accountant to explore Williams's financial activities. It's something we'd been doing for decades, along with hiring private investigators to keep track of his whereabouts. Williams had been living in Jacksonville, Florida, with a retired school teacher whom he married while still in prison. He had $500 in a bank account. I could've attached it to the civil judgment, but it would've cost more than that just to get it.

There was $750,000 in cash in the ransom bag. Williams was arrested with $10,300 in matching bills on his person. Another $28,000 was found in the mobile home. He bought the mobile home for $20,000 in cash (plus a $500 tip), and we believe he spent another $100,000 on a home in Florida. Then there was the $10,000 donation to the Organization of African Unity, which I got back. The rest is unaccounted for.

We deposed Williams prior to the deal that sprang him from prison. We pressed him hard about the missing money. I asked Buddy Martin, our company accountant, to attend the deposition in the hopes that some piece of information would lead us to the money. That Williams would slip, and we could dig it up. But it didn't happen. Whatever they asked him, Williams would just lie. It was nothing to him. Everybody knew it.

We tried many times and many ways. I spent a lot of money. I hired companies to help us track it down. We searched under Williams and Berkley's names, their aliases, wives, girlfriends, and friends' names—even their children's. McGuire dedicated huge amounts of his personal time to cracking the mystery. He was so dedicated. For me it wasn't so much about the money itself but what it might be used for; namely, funding future terrorist activities or fueling violent radicalism that might harm other innocents.

Still, we didn't find anything. If money was left to their wives or kids, there was probably no way of getting it. Williams died with nothing in his estate. He and Berkley took the secret to their graves.

There were at least three kidnappers, maybe four. Perhaps they split the money and lived well for a few years. There weren't computers in those days to electronically follow money. Unless they were caught red-handed, like Williams, the bills would circulate and recirculate beyond detection. And when the one-hundred-dollar bills became obsolete due to new bill designs, banks would trade them out for new ones, and the old bills would be destroyed. It's a common practice meant to prevent counterfeiting.

Williams could have gone to Las Vegas and exchanged $5,000 for an equal amount in gambling chips, only to change them out again and receive new bills. The ransom bills would've been dispersed the same day, then exponentially more with each passing day making them impossible to trace in a short amount of time.

McGuire was convinced Williams used a large amount of the ransom to buy real estate. He searched county clerks of court offices around the country—New York, New Jersey, California, Florida—to see if he could identify any property ownership leads. He researched names, aliases, and anything else that he could think of.

McCarty thought the money may have been stashed offshore in the U.S. Virgin Islands. Williams's father lived there, and he had traveled throughout the Caribbean extensively. Corporations and wealthy individuals have long sought tax shelters and opaque banking protections in the Virgin Islands.

There was good reason to believe it was Williams's final destination. None of it could be proved, but McCarty hypothesized that Williams was heading for Mexico when he was arrested in Barstow, California. The mobile home he was driving pulled a four-wheel drive International TravelAll that could better handle rough terrain as he tacked further and further east.

Barstow is also a road junction where Interstates 10 and 15 intersect. If Williams took I-10 due east, he'd eventually land back in Jacksonville. He could hide out there or puddle-jump down through the Caribbean to the Virgin Islands.

Another theory involves John Wesley Ford, a university professor and Florida resident who allegedly helped Williams purchase his mobile home. Ford made at least one real estate purchase around the same time. Was he one of the kidnappers? There wasn't enough evidence to indict him along with Williams and Berkley, but McGuire strongly suspected his involvement.

I would've liked to know more about Berkley's involvement. He worked for me for all those years, and I never would've imagined him capable of such depravity. I knew Williams was the Keeper, but was Berkley in the tenement apartment? He fingered me as the target but what else, exactly?

Today, the ransom money would be worth more than $4 million. It'd be an enormous boon for current and future members of my family, but I believe it's gone. McCarty and McGuire do too. It's not buried in a treasure box or hidden between a canvas painting and its frame. It's gone. I only hope it wasn't used to hurt other people or support terrorist activities outside the country.

* * *

TODAY MOST PEOPLE DON'T MENTION my kidnapping to me, but it used to be unavoidable. We had to learn to deal with people making inappropriate comments or bringing it up as a topic of conversation at awkward and uncomfortable times.

"Do you know what happened to Jack and Janet years ago? Jack was kidnapped. Isn't that wild?"

It's such a personal thing to be abused like we were. I tried not to let it bother me and ignored those moments the best I could. But given the national attention my case received and the size of the ransom, it's inevitable that people are curious. Perhaps this book will help answer many of their questions.

Janet and I vowed to spend our remaining days working part-time, traveling, and enjoying life together. We've been through so much, and we've dealt with severe health issues. But I'd be lying if I didn't admit that the kidnapping still hovers like an apparition. To this day we never go eight hours without checking on each other, talking on the phone, each knowing the other is safe. If business travel or life has us in separate locations, we talk frequently...that terrifying week in 1974 left a permanent scar.

There's an old picture of Janet from the newspaper the night I was released near JFK. It still brings tears to my eyes. Her fear, anger, and compassion for me reside in her expression. That old black and white clipping, now patinaed with age, shows in one faded look the hell she endured. Today I marvel at her strength in pushing past the pain to defiantly live a life of joy and gratitude.

As for our children, Marc, Michael, and Jaime, I am thankful to say that they are all living healthy, successful lives—and have made us proud grandparents! I wish I could say that the trauma I endured didn't affect my ability to be emotionally available and strong for my children throughout every phase of their lives, but that wouldn't be honest. Even my daughter, Jaime, who had not been born when my kidnapping occurred, has experienced that pain in the form of my emotional distance at times. It wasn't for a lack of love; to the contrary, it was because I was afraid and unsure how to love freely. I never even told her about my abduction. When she was in middle school, and her class was reading the book, *The Face on the Milk Carton*, Jaime shared with her mother that she was so troubled and upset by the book's subject matter, that Janet had to tell her what had happened in our family. Her dad had been kidnapped. Later, she stumbled on an old news article about it while researching microfiche in the library. I had hoped to protect her innocence and sense of safety. Naïve? Maybe. But I know my intentions were pure and rooted in love for her.

My pain elevator goes down farther than I want my children to know. It's not a ride I want to take them on. I can descend into the abyss at the mere press of an emotional button. They don't need that.

* * *

JANET AND I MADE AN EVERLASTING PACT to seek joy, make memories with our children and grandchildren, and savor the smiles in between. It took many years and countless therapy sessions to get to this point, but we're here now. Together.

In the closet I vowed to hang on for my wife and children, but I still marvel at how Janet mustered the courage to walk straight into danger on the slim chance that doing so might bring me back home alive. I don't know how she did it. She had the kids. She had the weight of all those FBI agents, police detectives, the media, our family, our friends, and the terror of dealing with militant criminals all on her shoulders. Yet she never wavered—not even when the FBI tested her resolve. Ending the horror all hinged on her. And she did it. My loving, beautiful Janet.

She is just as radiant today as she was on August 21, 1965—the day we were married. I look at her daily and wonder how I got so damn lucky. I wouldn't be here without you, Janet. You saved my life. I love you.

Acknowledgments

I was blessed directly after this ordeal to meet and be deeply involved with so many smart, dedicated, and compassionate professionals—some of whom have become part of our extended family.

My brothers, Eddie and Buddy; my father, Joe; and my beloved wife, Janet, are the reason I am still here to write this book. What they endured the week of my captivity is way beyond anything you can imagine or describe, especially with two very young children to care for. I'd also like to thank Arnold and Sylvia Rosenberg.

A special thank you to Helen and Harvey Teich for being by my father's side and caring for him during the week of my abduction.

Judge Jules "Jed" Orenstein, then a young Nassau County assistant district attorney, was instrumental in getting the investigation started. When he received the panicked call from Janet, he immediately connected with the NCPD to report me missing. Detective Chief Ed Curran and Deputy Inspector Dan Guido took the lead and were totally involved with my family throughout. They were among the most professional in law enforcement that I have had the honor to know.

Buddy Martin, our accountant, financial advisor, and friend, was instrumental working with the family and the bank in obtaining the ransom money, as was Martin Rosen, our attorney and friend, who provided expert financial and legal advice.

Detective Sergeant Frank Spinelli, NCPD and FBI Special Agents Joe Conely and Margot Dennedy moved into our house twenty-four/seven that week with Janet. Margot has become part of our extended family as well. The night I was released I spent being debriefed with FBI Special Agent Fred Behrends, whom I spent many subsequent days and hours with during the course of the investigation, including the hypnosis session. NCPD Chief Owens and Deputy Inspector Dan Guido were also present for my initial debriefing.

I must acknowledge Joan and Barry Kay. They came as soon as Janet called and stayed during the day with her. They allowed the FBI, NCPD, Buddy, and Janet to go to their house to talk privately whenever necessary. They also came every night to support and comfort Janet.

I must also acknowledge my former sister-in-law, Lois Teich, and my brother, Buddy. Lois and Buddy didn't have any children at that time and always treated our son, Marc, as a son. They had him stay at their house for four days. Lois stopped what she was doing to help in any way that she could. Janet doesn't know what she would have done without them. Also, Seymour and Phyllis Cohen, who came to look for me that fateful night and gave the family comfort and support during that horrific week.

I must give special note to Deputy Inspector Danny Guido, with whom I also spent numerous days and hours over the course of two years. Dan was the brightest person in law enforcement that I had the honor to know.

Special thanks to Assistant FBI Director John Malone and Supervising Agent Henry Schutz, who assigned scores of agents to the case.

FBI agents who were heavily involved in the investigation were Damon Taylor, Matt Mullin, Bill Stolarski, and especially Doug Ball, who investigated and arrested Richard Williams in California.

Detective Sergeant Dick McGuire (my personal hero) spent over two years full-time on the case, after which, his wife, Irene, was happy to be able to see him again! Dick was hand-selected by Dan Guido to lead the investigation and was instrumental in solving the case. Dick has become part of our extended family.

NCPD detectives who were instrumental during the investigation include Det. William Noble, Det. Charles Frass, Det. Lt. Saverto

Soldo, Det. James Moran, and Det. James Magee. My thanks to all of these professionals. Thank you to Det. Jim Garvey, who spent months protecting me. Also, a special thanks to the NCPD lab that did amazing work during the investigation and preparing for trial.

Thank you to our NCPD security team—Dennis Delay, Charles Clark, Robert Bentivegna, John Farco, and the leader, Joe Polimine, who has become part of our extended family. This team was exceptional and with us nearly a year. Thank you also to the thirty detectives in the 6th squad who rotated shifts to protect our family.

Denis Dillon, Nassau County District Attorney, and his staff did an amazing, very professional, and most difficult job in the prosecution of this case.

Judge Alexander Vitale presided over a most difficult trial, the longest in Nassau County history up to that time. We are grateful for his wisdom and professionalism.

Henry Devine, Chief Assistant DA, selected the dynamic, dedicated, young ADA Ed McCarty to prosecute the most difficult case in State Supreme Court. Ed later went on to become a State Supreme Court Judge and then a Surrogate Judge. Our sincere thanks to all for an exceptional job.

I must also acknowledge all my employees at our company, Acme Steel Door & Partition, who knew I was missing but didn't know any specifics and prayed for me.

I could not have even thought of doing this book without the expert advice, talent, and wisdom of Will Patrick, Michelle Hall, and Wynton Hall. Will and Wynton were able to digest this very complicated story into timelines, facts, and conclusions. And Michelle kept us on track during this difficult and all-consuming project. Both my wife, Janet, and I thank Wynton for all he has done for us in over a year of working together.

As there were so many people involved, if I was remiss in leaving anyone out, please accept my sincerest apologies.

With the publication of this book and the detailed information about the crime in it, I hope that there may be renewed interest in solving it. Accordingly, I am offering to pay $50,000 for information that leads to the return of a significant portion of the ransom money or the arrest and conviction of additional participants in the crime. If you have information about the crime, please contact Jacknap, Box 4155, 511 Avenue of the Americas, New York, NY 10011.

If any ransom money is recovered as a result of this offer, I will donate it to The Federal Law Enforcement Foundation, whose primary mission is to provide financial assistance to all Federal and local law enforcement.

About the Author

J ack Teich is a serial entrepreneur, philanthropist, and the proud grandfather of five and the father of three. An avid art collector, Teich was the president of Acme Architectural Products, a family business that manufactured commercial construction materials. Today, he is the president of Whitehead Company, a real estate investment company specializing in commercial property in New York and Pennsylvania, as well as a partner in Jubilee Restaurant Group. A member of numerous executive boards and international organizations like Young Presidents Organization (YPO), Chief Executive Organization (CEO), and the Friars Club, Jack is a graduate of American University in Washington, D.C., and served in the United States Coast Guard. He lives with his wife Janet Teich, a noted sculptor, in New York.